Houghton
Mifflin
Harcourt

CALIFORNIA
MATH
Expressions
Common Core

Dr. Karen C. Fuson

GRADE

1

Volume 2

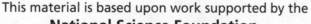

This material is based upon work supported by the
National Science Foundation
under Grant Numbers
ESI-9816320, REC-9806020, and RED-935373.

Any opinions, findings, and conclusions, or recommendations expressed in this material
are those of the author and do not necessarily reflect the views of the National Science Foundation.

VOLUME 2 CONTENTS

UNIT 5 Place Value Situations

UNIT 6 Comparisons and Data

UNIT 7 Geometry, Measurement, and Equal Shares

© Houghton Mifflin Harcourt Publishing Company

* This lesson consists only of activities from the Teacher Edition.

UNIT 8 Two-Digit Addition

BIG IDEA	Add 2-Digit Numbers

Student Resources

* This lesson consists only of activities from the Teacher Edition.

Dear Family:

In the previous unit, your child learned the Make a Ten strategy to find teen totals. Now, your child builds on previous knowledge to use make a ten to find an unknown partner. The Make a Ten strategy is explained below.

In a teen addition problem such as 9 + 5, children break apart the lesser number to make a ten with the greater number. Because 9 + 1 = 10, they break apart 5 into 1 + 4. Then they add the extra 4 onto 10 to find the total. A similar method is used to find unknown partners with teen totals. Children look for ways to make a ten because it is easier to add onto 10.

In the *Math Expressions* program, Make-a-Ten Cards help children use this method. Each card has a problem on the front. The back shows the answer and illustrates the Make a Ten strategy using pictures of dots. Below the pictures are corresponding numbers to help children understand how to make a ten. Practice the method with your child. As you continue to practice the Make a Ten strategy with your child, your child will become more adept at using mental math.

If you have any question about the Make a Ten strategy, please contact me.

Sincerely,
Your child's teacher

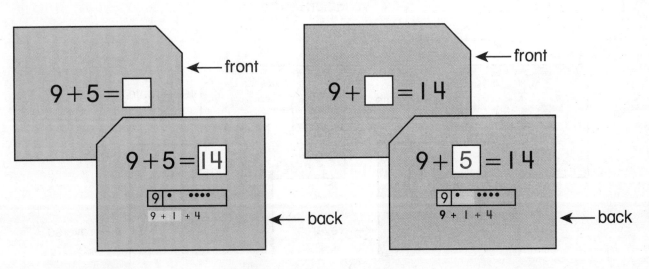

Make-a-Ten Cards

© Houghton Mifflin Harcourt Publishing Company

 CA CC

Unit 5 addresses the following standards from the *Common Core State Standards for Mathematics with California Additions*: 1.OA.1, 1.OA.2, 1.OA.3, 1.OA.4, 1.OA.5, 1.OA.6, 1.OA.8, 1.NBT.1, 1.NBT.2, 1.NBT.2c, 1.NBT.4, 1.NBT.5, 1.NBT.6 and all Mathematical Practices.

Estimada familia:

En la unidad anterior, su niño aprendió la Estrategia hacer decenas para hallar totales de números de 11 a 19. Ahora, su niño ampliará esos conocimientos previos y hará decenas para hallar una parte desconocida. La Estrategia hacer decenas se explica debajo.

En una suma con números de 11 a 19, tal como 9 + 5, los niños separan el número menor para formar una decena con el número mayor. Como 9 + 1 = 10, separan el 5 en 1 + 4. Luego suman al 10 los 4 que sobran para hallar el total. Un método semejante se usa para hallar partes desconocidas con totales de números de 11 a 19. Los niños buscan maneras de formar una decena porque es más fácil sumar con 10.

En el programa *Math Expressions* las tarjetas de hacer decenas ayudan a los niños a usar este método. Cada tarjeta tiene un problema en el frente. En el reverso se muestra la respuesta y se ilustra la Estrategia hacer decenas mediante dibujos de puntos. Debajo de los dibujos están los números correspondientes para ayudar a los niños a comprender cómo se hace una decena. Practique el método con su niño. A medida que practican la estrategia, su niño adquirirá mayor dominio del cálculo mental.

Si tiene alguna pregunta sobre la Estrategia hacer decenas, por favor comuníquese conmigo.

Atentamente,
El maestro de su niño

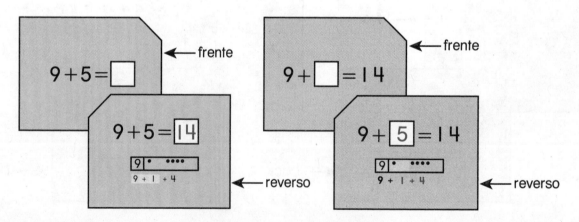

Tarjetas de hacer decenas

CA CC

En la Unidad 5 se aplican los siguientes estándares auxiliares, contenidos en los *Estándares estatales comunes de matemáticas con adiciones para California*: **1.OA.1, 1.OA.2, 1.OA.3, 1.OA.4, 1.OA.5, 1.OA.6, 1.OA.8, 1.NBT.1, 1.NBT.2, 1.NBT.2c, 1.NBT.4, 1.NBT.5, 1.NBT.6** y todos los de prácticas matemáticas.

$7 + \boxed{} = 16$

$6 + \boxed{} = 15$

$7 + \boxed{} = 11$

$8 + \boxed{} = 12$

$9 + \boxed{} = 13$

$6 + \boxed{} = 11$

$7 + \boxed{} = 12$

$8 + \boxed{} = 13$

$9 + \boxed{} = 14$

$5 + \boxed{} = 11$

$9 + \boxed{} = 18$

$7 + \boxed{} = 13$

$8 + \boxed{} = 14$

$9 + \boxed{} = 15$

$4 + \boxed{} = 11$

$7 + \boxed{4} = 11$

7 ••• •
7 + 3 + 1

$6 + \boxed{9} = 15$

6 •••• •••••
6 + 4 + 5

$7 + \boxed{9} = 16$

7 ••• ••••••
7 + 3 + 6

$6 + \boxed{5} = 11$

6 •••• •
6 + 4 + 1

$9 + \boxed{4} = 13$

9 • •••
9 + 1 + 3

$8 + \boxed{4} = 12$

8 •• ••
8 + 2 + 2

$9 + \boxed{5} = 14$

9 • ••••
9 + 1 + 4

$8 + \boxed{5} = 13$

8 •• •••
8 + 2 + 3

$7 + \boxed{5} = 12$

7 ••• ••
7 + 3 + 2

$7 + \boxed{6} = 13$

7 ••• •••
7 + 3 + 3

$9 + \boxed{9} = 18$

9 • ••••••••
9 + 1 + 8

$5 + \boxed{6} = 11$

5 ••••• •
5 + 5 + 1

$4 + \boxed{7} = 11$

4 •••••• •
4 + 6 + 1

$9 + \boxed{6} = 15$

9 • •••••
9 + 1 + 5

$8 + \boxed{6} = 14$

8 •• ••••
8 + 2 + 4

Purple Make-a-Ten Cards

$5 + \boxed{} = 12$ $6 + \boxed{} = 13$ $8 + \boxed{} = 17$

$8 + \boxed{} = 15$ $9 + \boxed{} = 16$ $3 + \boxed{} = 11$

$4 + \boxed{} = 12$ $5 + \boxed{} = 13$ $6 + \boxed{} = 14$

$7 + \boxed{} = 15$ $8 + \boxed{} = 16$ $9 + \boxed{} = 17$

$3 + \boxed{} = 12$ $4 + \boxed{} = 13$ $5 + \boxed{} = 14$

$$8 + \boxed{9} = 17$$

8 | •• ••••
8 + 2 + 7

$$6 + \boxed{7} = 13$$

6 | •••• •••
6 + 4 + 3

$$5 + \boxed{7} = 12$$

5 | ••••• ••
5 + 5 + 2

$$3 + \boxed{8} = 11$$

3 | ••••••• •
3 + 7 + 1

$$9 + \boxed{7} = 16$$

9 | • •••••
9 + 1 + 6

$$8 + \boxed{7} = 15$$

8 | •• •••••
8 + 2 + 5

$$6 + \boxed{8} = 14$$

6 | •••• ••••
6 + 4 + 4

$$5 + \boxed{8} = 13$$

5 | ••••• •••
5 + 5 + 3

$$4 + \boxed{8} = 12$$

4 | •••••• ••
4 + 6 + 2

$$9 + \boxed{8} = 17$$

9 | • •••••••
9 + 1 + 7

$$8 + \boxed{8} = 16$$

8 | •• ••••••
8 + 2 + 6

$$7 + \boxed{8} = 15$$

7 | ••• •••••
7 + 3 + 5

$$5 + \boxed{9} = 14$$

5 | ••••• ••••
5 + 5 + 4

$$4 + \boxed{9} = 13$$

4 | •••••• •••
4 + 6 + 3

$$3 + \boxed{9} = 12$$

3 | ••••••• ••
3 + 7 + 2

Purple Make-a-Ten Cards

Match the equation with the picture that shows
how to use the Make a Ten strategy to solve.
Write the **unknown partner**.

1. $8 + \boxed{} = 12$

$\boxed{9 \mid \bullet \quad\quad \bullet\bullet}$

2. $9 + \boxed{} = 15$

$\boxed{7 \mid \bullet\bullet\bullet \quad \bullet\bullet}$

3. $7 + \boxed{} = 12$

$\boxed{9 \mid \bullet \quad\quad \bullet}$

4. $8 + \boxed{} = 14$

$\boxed{8 \mid \bullet\bullet \quad\quad \bullet\bullet}$

5. $9 + \boxed{} = 12$

$\boxed{8 \mid \bullet\bullet \quad\quad \bullet\bullet\bullet\bullet}$

6. $8 + \boxed{} = 15$

$\boxed{9 \mid \bullet \quad\quad \bullet\bullet\bullet\bullet\bullet}$

7. $9 + \boxed{} = 11$

$\boxed{9 \mid \bullet \quad\quad \bullet\bullet\bullet\bullet\bullet\bullet\bullet}$

8. $9 + \boxed{} = 17$

$\boxed{8 \mid \bullet\bullet \quad\quad \bullet\bullet\bullet\bullet\bullet}$

9. $7 + \boxed{} = 11$

$\boxed{7 \mid \bullet\bullet\bullet \quad\quad \bullet}$

Solve the story problem.

---

10. Some birds are in a tree. 5 more birds fly into the tree. Now there are 13 birds. How many birds were in the tree before?

tree

[ ] _____
label

---

11. 14 cats are black or white. 8 cats are black. How many cats are white?

cat

[ ] _____
label

---

12. 10 kites are big. 10 kites are small. How many kites are there?

kite

[ ] _____
label

---

13. Juan has 8 books. Meg brings more books. Now there are 17 books. How many books does Meg bring?

book

[ ] _____
label

© Houghton Mifflin Harcourt Publishing Company

Unknown Partners with Teen Totals

$15 - 6 = \boxed{}$ $16 - 7 = \boxed{}$ $11 - 7 = \boxed{}$

$12 - 8 = \boxed{}$ $13 - 9 = \boxed{}$ $11 - 6 = \boxed{}$

$12 - 7 = \boxed{}$ $13 - 8 = \boxed{}$ $14 - 9 = \boxed{}$

$11 - 5 = \boxed{}$ $17 - 8 = \boxed{}$ $13 - 7 = \boxed{}$

$14 - 8 = \boxed{}$ $15 - 9 = \boxed{}$ $11 - 4 = \boxed{}$

$11 - 7 = \boxed{4}$

7 | ••• •
7 + 3 + 1

$16 - 7 = \boxed{9}$

7 | ••• •••••
7 + 3 + 6

$15 - 6 = \boxed{9}$

6 | •••• •••••
6 + 4 + 5

$11 - 6 = \boxed{5}$

6 | •••• •
6 + 4 + 1

$13 - 9 = \boxed{4}$

9 | • •••
9 + 1 + 3

$12 - 8 = \boxed{4}$

8 | •• ••
8 + 2 + 2

$14 - 9 = \boxed{5}$

9 | • ••••
9 + 1 + 4

$13 - 8 = \boxed{5}$

8 | •• •••
8 + 2 + 3

$12 - 7 = \boxed{5}$

7 | ••• ••
7 + 3 + 2

$13 - 7 = \boxed{6}$

7 | ••• •••
7 + 3 + 3

$17 - 8 = \boxed{9}$

8 | •• •••••••
8 + 2 + 7

$11 - 5 = \boxed{6}$

5 | ••••• •
5 + 5 + 1

$11 - 4 = \boxed{7}$

4 | •••• •
4 + 6 + 1

$15 - 9 = \boxed{6}$

9 | • •••••
9 + 1 + 5

$14 - 8 = \boxed{6}$

8 | •• ••••
8 + 2 + 4

Blue Make-a-Ten Cards

$12 - 5 = \square$ $13 - 6 = \square$ $18 - 9 = \square$

$15 - 8 = \square$ $16 - 9 = \square$ $11 - 3 = \square$

$12 - 4 = \square$ $13 - 5 = \square$ $14 - 6 = \square$

$15 - 7 = \square$ $16 - 8 = \square$ $17 - 9 = \square$

$12 - 3 = \square$ $13 - 4 = \square$ $14 - 5 = \square$

$18 - 9 =$ $\boxed{9}$

$\boxed{9}$ • ••• ••••

9 + 1 + 8

$13 - 6 =$ $\boxed{7}$

$\boxed{6}$ •••• •••

6 + 4 + 3

$12 - 5 =$ $\boxed{7}$

$\boxed{5}$ ••••• ••

5 + 5 + 2

$11 - 3 =$ $\boxed{8}$

$\boxed{3}$ ••• •••• •

3 + 7 + 1

$16 - 9 =$ $\boxed{7}$

$\boxed{9}$ • ••••••

9 + 1 + 6

$15 - 8 =$ $\boxed{7}$

$\boxed{8}$ •• •••••

8 + 2 + 5

$14 - 6 =$ $\boxed{8}$

$\boxed{6}$ •••• ••••

6 + 4 + 4

$13 - 5 =$ $\boxed{8}$

$\boxed{5}$ ••••• •••

5 + 5 + 3

$12 - 4 =$ $\boxed{8}$

$\boxed{4}$ •••• ••

4 + 6 + 2

$17 - 9 =$ $\boxed{8}$

$\boxed{9}$ • ••••••

9 + 1 + 7

$16 - 8 =$ $\boxed{8}$

$\boxed{8}$ •• ••••••

8 + 2 + 6

$15 - 7 =$ $\boxed{8}$

$\boxed{7}$ ••• •••••

7 + 3 + 5

$14 - 5 =$ $\boxed{9}$

$\boxed{5}$ ••••• ••••

5 + 5 + 4

$13 - 4 =$ $\boxed{9}$

$\boxed{4}$ •••• •••

4 + 6 + 3

$12 - 3 =$ $\boxed{9}$

$\boxed{3}$ ••• •• ••

3 + 7 + 2

Blue Make-a-Ten Cards

Name _____

CA CC Content Standards **1.OA.4, 1.OA.5, 1.OA.6**
Mathematical Practices **MP.2, MP.6**

Match the equation with the picture that shows how to use the Make a Ten strategy to solve.

1. $12 - 8 =$ ☐ | 7 | ● ● ●   ● ● ● |

2. $14 - 9 =$ ☐ | 8 | ● ●   ● ● ● ● |

3. $13 - 7 =$ ☐ | 8 | ● ●   ● ● |

4. $15 - 8 =$ ☐ | 7 | ● ● ●   ● ● |

5. $14 - 8 =$ ☐ | 9 | ●   ● ● ● ● |

6. $12 - 7 =$ ☐ | 6 | ● ● ● ●   ● ● ● ● |

7. $11 - 8 =$ ☐ | 8 | ● ●   ● ● ● ● ● |

8. $14 - 6 =$ ☐ | 9 | ●   ● |

9. $11 - 9 =$ ☐ | 8 | ● ●   ● |

	Step 1	Step 2
$14 - 6 = \boxed{8}$ $\;\;\;\;\diagdown\diagup$ $\;\;4\;\;\;\;\;2$	$14 - 4 = 10$	$10 - 2 = 8$

Subtract.

10. $15 - 8 = \boxed{}$

11. $13 - 4 = \boxed{}$

12. $12 - 9 = \boxed{}$

13. $17 - 9 = \boxed{}$

CA CC Content Standards **1.OA.1, 1.OA.6, 1.OA.8**
Mathematical Practices **MP.2, MP.6**

Solve the story problem.

Show your work. Use drawings, numbers, or words.

---

1. 17 berries are in a bowl. 9 are red and the rest are purple. How many berries are purple?

    bowl

    ☐ _____
    label

---

2. I draw some stars. 8 are large and 7 are small. How many stars do I draw?

    star

    ☐ _____
    label

---

3. There are 14 puppies. Some are brown and some are black. How many brown and black puppies could there be?
    Show three answers.

    puppy

    ☐ brown puppies and ☐ black puppies

    or ☐ brown puppies and ☐ black puppies

    or ☐ brown puppies and ☐ black puppies

Name _____

Solve the story problem.

Show your work. Use drawings, numbers, or words.

---

4. 15 frogs are by the pond. 9 hop away. How many frogs are there now?

pond

☐ _____
    label

---

5. 16 butterflies are in the garden. Some fly away. There are 8 left. How many butterflies fly away?

butterflies

☐ _____
    label

---

6. Some grapes are in a bowl. I eat 6 of them. Now there are 7 grapes. How many grapes were in the bowl before?

grapes

☐ _____
    label

---

7. There are 12 horses in a field. Some run away. Now there are 5 horses. How many horses run away?

horse

☐ _____
    label

Mixed Practice with Teen Problems

Name _____

CA CC Content Standards **1.OA.5, 1.OA.6, 1.OA.8**
Mathematical Practices **MP.2, MP.8**

Match the equation with the picture that shows
how to use the Make a Ten strategy to solve.

1. $8 +$ ☐ $= 14$

| 8 | ••   • |

2. $7 + 5 =$ ☐

| 6 | •••••   ••••• |

3. $8 + 3 =$ ☐

| 8 | ••   •••• |

4. $6 +$ ☐ $= 15$

| 7 | •••   ••• |

5. $9 +$ ☐ $= 18$

| 9 | •   ••••• |

6. $9 +$ ☐ $= 15$

| 8 | ••   •• |

7. $8 + 4 =$ ☐

| 9 | •   •••••••• |

8. $7 + 6 =$ ☐

| 7 | •••   •• |

9. Ring the picture above that shows
how to use the Make a Ten strategy
to solve the equation.

$13 - 7 =$ ☐

Name

Add.

10. $9 + 3 =$ ☐   11. $7 + 8 =$ ☐   12. $7 + 5 =$ ☐

13. $10 + 10 =$ ☐   14. $8 + 5 =$ ☐   15. $2 + 9 =$ ☐

16. $11 + 9 =$ ☐   17. $12 + 7 =$ ☐   18. $8 + 12 =$ ☐

Find the unknown partner.

19. $9 +$ ☐ $= 14$ 20. $10 +$ ☐ $= 19$ 21. $6 +$ ☐ $= 13$

22. ☐ $+ 4 = 12$ 23. ☐ $+ 8 = 11$ 24. ☐ $+ 6 = 15$

Subtract.

25. $11 - 2 =$ ☐   26. $14 - 6 =$ ☐   27. $13 - 9 =$ ☐

28. $16 - 8 =$ ☐   29. $13 - 7 =$ ☐   30. $12 - 5 =$ ☐

PATH to FLUENCY Subtract.

1. $10 - 8 =$ ☐   2. $7 - 1 =$ ☐   3. $6 - 6 =$ ☐

4. $9 - 7 =$ ☐   5. $8 - 4 =$ ☐   6. $10 - 6 =$ ☐

Small Group Practice with Teen Problems

1. Rosa reads 8 stories. Tim reads 5 stories.
   How many stories do they read in all?

2. Rosa reads 8 stories. Tim also reads some stories.
   They read 13 stories in all. How many stories
   does Tim read?

3. Rosa reads some stories. Tim reads 5 stories.
   They read 13 stories in all. How many stories
   does Rosa read?

Some crayons are in a box.
I take 6 crayons out.
Now there are 9 crayons in the box.
How many crayons were in the box before?

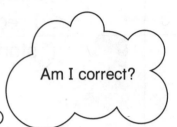

Am I correct?

4. Look at what Puzzled Penguin wrote.

| 9 | − | 6 | = | 3 |

| 3 | crayons

5. Help Puzzled Penguin.

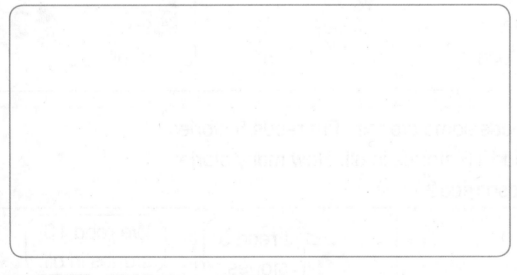

| | − | | = | |

| | crayons

Teen Problems with Various Unknowns

Name _____

CA CC Content Standards **1.OA.2, 1.OA.3**
Mathematical Practices **MP.4, MP.5**

Model and solve the story problem.
Color to show your model.
Cross out the cubes you do not use.

1. There are 6 red pencils, 5 yellow pencils,
   and 7 green pencils in a cup.
   How many pencils are in the cup?

cup

☐○

☐
_____
label

2. I have 4 white fish, 2 black fish,
   and 6 orange fish in my fish tank.
   How many fish are in my fish tank?

fish

☐○

☐
_____
label

3. There are 3 pears on the table, 10 pears
   in a basket, and 7 pears in a bowl.
   How many pears are there?

pear

☐○

☐
_____
label

Solve the story problem.

Show your work. Use drawings, numbers, or words.

4. There are 5 red crayons, 9 blue crayons, and 1 yellow crayon on the table. How many crayons are on the table?

crayon

☐ _____
label

5. Charlie sees 4 books on a desk, 6 books on a shelf, and 8 books on a cart. How many books does Charlie see?

desk

☐ _____
label

6. Gina finds 7 seashells. Paul finds 6 seashells. Lee finds 3 seashells. How many seashells do they find altogether?

seashell

☐ _____
label

Problems with Three Addends

VOCABULARY
10-group

I. Ring **10-groups**. Count by tens and ones.
Write the number.

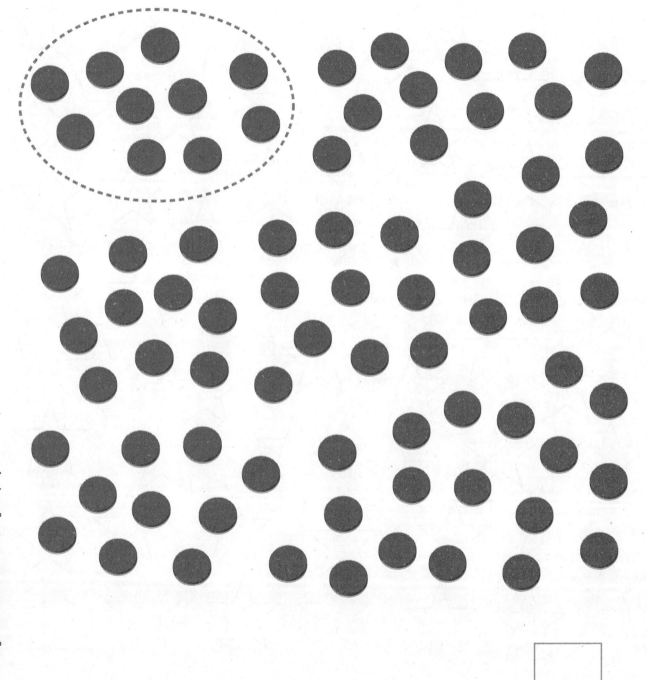

2. Color each 10-group a different color.
Count by tens and ones. Write the number.

Count with Groups of 10

Family Letter

Content Overview

Dear Family:

The next several lessons of this unit build upon what the class learned previously about tens and ones. The Hundred Grid is a tool that allows children to see 10-based patterns in sequence. Seeing numbers in the ordered rows and columns of the Hundred Grid helps children better understand number relationships as they:

- continue to practice with 10-groups, adding tens to any 2-digit number, with totals to 100;
- explore 2-digit subtraction, subtracting tens from decade numbers;
- connect what they know about 10-partners to now find 100-partners.

1	11	21	31	41	51	61	71	81	91
2	12	22	32	42	52	62	72	82	92
3	13	23	33	43	53	63	73	83	93
4	14	24	34	44	54	64	74	84	94
5	15	25	35	45	55	65	75	85	95
6	16	26	36	46	56	66	76	86	96
7	17	27	37	47	57	67	77	87	97
8	18	28	38	48	58	68	78	88	98
9	19	29	39	49	59	69	79	89	99
10	20	30	40	50	60	70	80	90	100

3 ooo
13 | ooo
23 || ooo
33 ||| ooo
43 |||| ooo
53 ||||| ooo
63 ||||| | ooo
73 ||||| || ooo
83 ||||| ||| ooo
93 ||||| |||| ooo

If you have any questions or problems, please contact me.

Sincerely,
Your child's teacher

CA CC

Unit 5 addresses the following standards from the *Common Core State Standards for Mathematics with California Additions*: **1.OA.1, 1.OA.2, 1.OA.3, 1.OA.4, 1.OA.5, 1.OA.6, 1.OA.8, 1.NBT.1, 1.NBT.2, 1.NBT.2c, 1.NBT.4, 1.NBT.5, 1.NBT.6** and all Mathematical Practices.

Un vistazo general al contenido

Estimada familia:

Las siguientes lecciones en esta unidad amplían lo que la clase aprendió anteriormente acerca de decenas y unidades. La Cuadrícula de 100 es un instrumento que permite observar patrones de base 10 en secuencia. Observar los números ordenados en hileras y columnas en la Cuadrícula de 100 ayudará a los niños a comprender mejor la relación entre los números mientras:

- continúan practicando con grupos de 10, sumando decenas a números de 2 dígitos con totales hasta 100;
- exploran la resta de números de 2 dígitos, restando decenas de números que terminan en cero;
- relacionan lo que saben acerca de las partes de 10 para hallar partes de 100.

1	11	21	31	41	51	61	71	81	91
2	12	22	32	42	52	62	72	82	92
3	13	23	33	43	53	63	73	83	93
4	14	24	34	44	54	64	74	84	94
5	15	25	35	45	55	65	75	85	95
6	16	26	36	46	56	66	76	86	96
7	17	27	37	47	57	67	77	87	97
8	18	28	38	48	58	68	78	88	98
9	19	29	39	49	59	69	79	89	99
10	20	30	40	50	60	70	80	90	100

3 ○○○
13 | ○○○
23 | | ○○○
33 | | | ○○○
43 | | | | ○○○
53 | | | | | ○○○
63 | | | | | | ○○○
73 | | | | | | | ○○○
83 | | | | | | | | ○○○
93 | | | | | | | | | ○○○

Si tiene alguna pregunta o algún comentario comuníquese conmigo.

Atentamente,
El maestro de su niño

CA CC

En la Unidad 5 se aplican los siguientes estándares auxiliares, contenidos en los *Estándares estatales comunes de matemáticas con adiciones para California*: 1.OA.1, 1.OA.2, 1.OA.3, 1.OA.4, 1.OA.5, 1.OA.6, 1.OA.8, 1.NBT.1, 1.NBT.2, 1.NBT.2c, 1.NBT.4, 1.NBT.5, 1.NBT.6 y todos los de prácticas matemáticas.

CA CC Content Standards **1.NBT.1, 1.NBT.2, 1.NBT.5**
Mathematical Practices **MP.5, MP.6, MP.7, MP.8**

1. Write the numbers 1–120 in **columns**.

1	11										
2											
10									100		120

Use the **grid** to find 10 more. Write the number.

2. 29   **3.** 72   **4.** 45   **5.** 90

Use the grid to find 10 less. Write the number.

6. 39   **7.** 72   **8.** 91   **9.** 20

VOCABULARY
row

10. Write the numbers 1–120 in **rows**.

1	2								10
11									
								100	
								120	

Use the grid to find 10 more.
Write the number.

Use the grid to find 10 less.
Write the number.

11. 63 [ ]   12. 51 [ ]   13. 83 [ ]   14. 51 [ ]

Make a Hundred Grid

Name

CA CC Content Standards **1.NBT.1, 1.NBT.2, 1.NBT.4, 1.NBT.5, 1.NBT.6** Mathematical Practices **MP.5, MP.7**

1. Listen to the directions.

1	11	21	31	41	51	61	71	81	91
2	12	22	32	42	52	62	72	82	92
3	13	23	33	43	53	63	73	83	93
4	14	24	34	44	54	64	74	84	94
5	15	25	35	45	55	65	75	85	95
6	16	26	36	46	56	66	76	86	96
7	17	27	37	47	57	67	77	87	97
8	18	28	38	48	58	68	78	88	98
9	19	29	39	49	59	69	79	89	99
10	20	30	40	50	60	70	80	90	100

Add tens.

2. 89 + 10 = ☐   **3.** 43 + 20 = ☐

4. 28 + 50 = ☐   **5.** 32 + 40 = ☐

6. 11 + 20 = ☐   **7.** 42 + 30 = ☐

8. 52 + 40 = ☐   **9.** 12 + 40 = ☐

10. 10 + 19 = ☐   **11.** 60 + 26 = ☐

Subtract tens.

12. 30 − 20 = ☐   **13.** 60 − 10 = ☐

14. 70 − 40 = ☐   **15.** 70 − 20 = ☐

16. 90 − 60 = ☐   **17.** 80 − 70 = ☐

18. 90 − 10 = ☐   **19.** 50 − 40 = ☐

Name

CA CC Content Standards 1.OA.6, 1.NBT.2c, 1.NBT.4, 1.NBT.6 Mathematical Practices MP.3, MP.6, MP.7

Solve.

1. $80 + 20 =$ ☐

2. $30 + 70 =$ ☐

3. $10 +$ ☐ $= 100$

4. $50 +$ ☐ $= 100$

5. $100 = 20 +$ ☐

6. $100 = 40 +$ ☐

7. $20 + 50 =$ ☐

8. $10 + 80 =$ ☐

9. $0 + 60 =$ ☐

10. $20 + 20 =$ ☐

11. $40 - 40 =$ ☐

12. $80 - 0 =$ ☐

13. $70 - 60 =$ ☐

14. $60 - 30 =$ ☐

15. $60 - 10 =$ ☐

$10 +$ ☐ $= 60$

16. $70 - 40 =$ ☐

$40 +$ ☐ $= 70$

17. $50 - 20 =$ ☐

$20 +$ ☐ $= 50$

18. $90 - 50 =$ ☐

$50 +$ ☐ $= 90$

Name

19. Look at what Puzzled Penguin wrote.

$$70 - 20 = \boxed{5}$$

Am I correct?

20. Help Puzzled Penguin.

$$70 - 20 = \boxed{}$$

PATH to FLUENCY Add.

1. $1 + 8 = \boxed{}$ 2. $5 + 4 = \boxed{}$ 3. $4 + 6 = \boxed{}$

4. $4 + 2 = \boxed{}$ 5. $7 + 1 = \boxed{}$ 6. $3 + 4 = \boxed{}$

PATH to FLUENCY Subtract.

7. $9 - 3 = \boxed{}$ 8. $6 - 1 = \boxed{}$ 9. $7 - 6 = \boxed{}$

10. $8 - 6 = \boxed{}$ 11. $10 - 3 = \boxed{}$ 12. $8 - 3 = \boxed{}$

Add and Subtract Multiples of 10

Name _____

CA CC Content Standards 1.OA.1, 1.OA.2
Mathematical Practices MP.1, MP.4, MP.5, MP.6, MP.7

► **Math and Gardening**

Use the picture.

Write the numbers to solve.

---

1. Casey helps gather fruit. How many
   pieces of fruit does Casey gather?

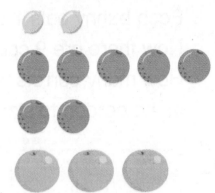

☐ 🍋 + ☐ 🍊 + ☐ 🍊 = ?

☐ + ☐ = ☐ pieces of fruit

---

2. Casey helps gather vegetables. How
   many vegetables does Casey gather?

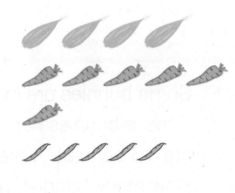

☐ 🌽 + ☐ 🥕 + ☐ 🫛 = ?

☐ + ☐ = ☐ vegetables

---

3. Casey helps gather flowers. How many
   flowers does Casey gather?

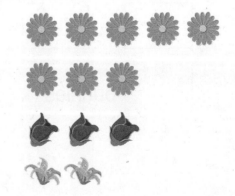

☐ 🌼 + ☐ 🌷 + ☐ 🌿 = ?

☐ + ☐ = ☐ flowers

Use the picture.
Write the numbers to solve.

---

4. Some carrots are in a garden.
   Each bunny eats 1 carrot.
   Now there are 9 carrots.
   How many carrots were
   in the garden to start?

   ☐ − ☐ = ☐

   ☐ carrots

---

5. Some bunnies are in a garden.
   7 more bunnies hop in. Now there
   are 13 bunnies in the garden.
   How many bunnies were
   in the garden before?

   ☐ + ☐ = ☐

   ☐ bunnies

Focus on Mathematical Practices

Match the box to the unknown partner.

1. $9 + \boxed{} = 15$　　2. $8 + \boxed{} = 15$　　3. $8 + \boxed{} = 17$

• 　　　　　　　　　　　• 　　　　　　　　　　　•

9 　　　　　　　　　　6 　　　　　　　　　　7

Solve the story problem.

4. Beth has 16 bagels. She gives 8 to her friends. How many bagels does Beth have now?

bagel

$\boxed{}$ _____
　　　　label

5. Meg has 6 books. Jen gives her some more books. Now Meg has 11 books. How many books does Jen give Meg?

book

$\boxed{}$ _____
　　　　label

6. Luis has 7 blue pens, 4 red pens, and 3 green pens. How many pens does Luis have?

pen

$\boxed{}$ _____
　　　　label

7. Is the sentence true? Choose Yes or No.

$14 - 8 = 5$ ○ Yes   ○ No

$16 - 7 = 9$ ○ Yes   ○ No

$17 - 9 = 8$ ○ Yes   ○ No

8. Start at 81. Count. Write the numbers through 110.

81	82	83							
91									

9. Draw a picture to solve the story problem.
Write a number sentence.
Answer the question.

There are 15 squirrels. Some are brown and
6 are gray. How many squirrels are brown?

☐ − ☐ = ☐

☐
_____
label

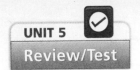
Solve.

10. 57 + 20 = [   ]   11. 13 + 60 = [   ]

12. 80 − 40 = [   ]   13. 70 − 50 = [   ]

14. 80 + [   ] = 100   15. 90 − [   ] = 70

Ring the number that makes the sentence true.

16. There are 9 red crayons, 3 green
crayons, and 7 blue crayons in the
box. How many crayons are in the box?

crayon

10

16   crayons are in the box.

19

17. There are 14 birds in a tree. Some
birds fly away. Now there are
6 birds. How many birds fly away?

bird

6

8   birds fly away.

14

18. There are 12 boys and girls on the bus.
    How many boys and girls can there be?
    Choose all possible answers.

    ○ 2 boys and 14 girls
    ○ 2 boys and 10 girls
    ○ 3 boys and 9 girls
    ○ 4 boys and 6 girls
    ○ 5 boys and 7 girls

19. Draw 20 to 30 more triangles.
    Ring 10-groups. Count by tens and ones.
    Write the numbers.

    △ △ △ △ △ △ △ △ △ △
    △ △ △ △ △ △ △ △ △ △
    △ △ △ △ △ △ △ △ △ △
    △ △ △ △ △ △ △ △ △ △
        △ △ △ △ △ △

    The number of triangles is ☐ .

    10 less is ☐ . 10 more is ☐ .

Family Letter

Content Overview

Dear Family:

Children begin this unit by learning to organize, represent, and interpret data with two and three categories.

In the example below, children sort apples and bananas and represent the data using circles. They ask and answer questions about the data and learn to express comparative statements completely.

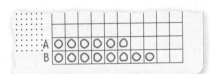

There are 2 more bananas than apples.

There are 2 fewer apples than bananas.

Later in the unit, children solve *Compare* story problems using comparison bars. Two examples are given below.

Jeremy has 10 crayons.
Amanda has 3 crayons.
How many more crayons does Jeremy have than Amanda?

J	10

A	3	?

Abby has 8 erasers.
Ramon has 6 more erasers than Abby has. How many erasers does Ramon have?

R	?

A	8	6

While working on homework, ask your child to explain to you how to use comparison bars to solve these types of story problems.

If you have any questions, please do not hesitate to contact me.

Sincerely,
Your child's teacher

CA CC

Unit 6 addresses the following standards from the *Common Core State Standards for Mathematics with California Additions*: **1.OA.1, 1.OA.2, 1.OA.6, 1.MD.4** and all Mathematical Practices.

Carta a la familia

Un vistazo general al contenido

Estimada familia:

Al comenzar esta unidad, los niños aprenderán a organizar, representar e interpretar datos de dos y tres categorías.

En el ejemplo de abajo, los niños clasifican manzanas y plátanos, y representan los datos usando círculos. Formulan y responden preguntas acerca de los datos y aprenden cómo expresar enunciados comparativos completos.

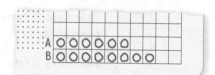

Hay 2 plátanos más que manzanas

Hay 2 manzanas menos que plátanos

Más adelante en la unidad, los niños resolverán problemas que requieran *comparar*, usando barras de comparación. Abajo se dan dos ejemplos.

Jeremy tiene 10 crayones.
Amanda tiene 3 crayones.
¿Cuántos crayones más que
Amanda tiene Jeremy?

J | 10
A | 3 | ?

Abby tiene 8 borradores.
Ramón tiene 6 borradores
más que Abby. ¿Cuántos
borradores tiene Ramón?

R | ?
A | 8 | 6

Mientras hace la tarea, pida a su niño que le explique cómo usar las barras de comparación para resolver este tipo de problemas.

Si tiene alguna pregunta, no dude en comunicarse conmigo.

Atentamente,
El maestro de su niño

 CA CC

En la Unidad 6 se aplican los siguientes estándares auxiliares, contenidos en los *Estándares estatales comunes de matemáticas con adiciones para California*: **1.OA.1, 1.OA.2, 1.OA.6, 1.MD.4** y todos los de prácticas matemáticas.

Explore Representing Data

Name _____

CA CC Content Standards 1.0A.1, 1.0A.2. 1.MD.4
Mathematical Practices MP.2, MP.8

VOCABULARY
sort

Cut out the cards.

Which bugs have legs?

Which bugs do not have legs?

Sort the bugs.

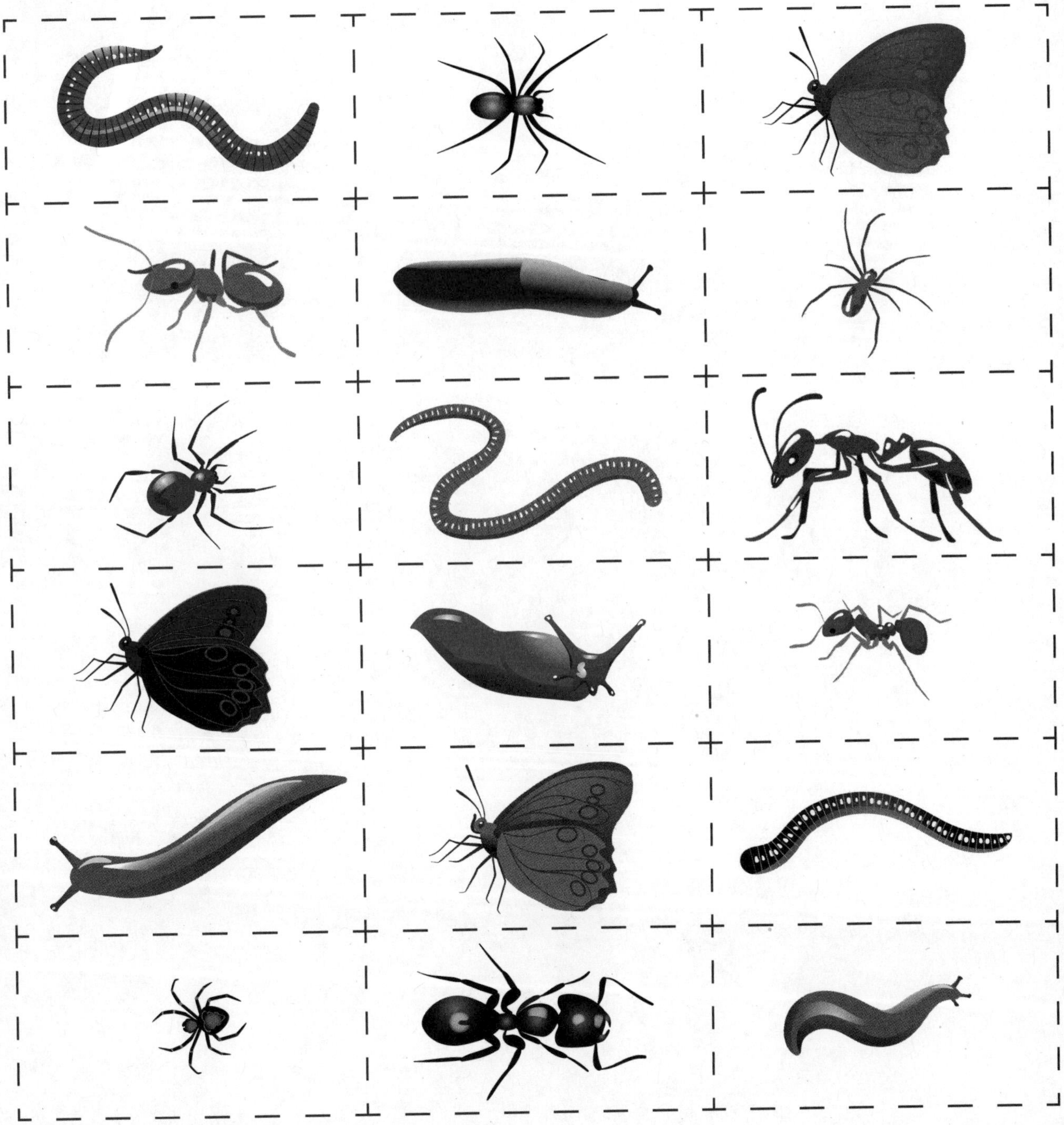

✂

Explore Representing Data **175**

Explore Representing Data

1. Use circles and 5-groups to record.
   Write how many in each group.

Legs	**No Legs**

Use the **data** to complete.

2. How many bugs in all? _____

3. Ring the group with **more** bugs.

4. Cross out the group with **fewer** bugs.

VOCABULARY
most
fewest

5. Use circles and 5-groups to record.
    Write how many in each group.

Brown	Red	Black

Use the data to complete.

6. How many bugs in all? _____

7. Ring the group with the **most** bugs.

8. Cross out the group with the **fewest** bugs.

Explore Representing Data

VOCABULARY
compare

1. Draw matching lines to **compare**.
   Complete the sentences.
   Ring the word **more** or **fewer**.

Mara

Todd

Mara has [ ] **more fewer** apples than Todd.

Todd has [ ] **more fewer** apples than Mara.

---

2. Each ant gets 1 crumb.
   How many more crumbs are needed? [ ]

3. Draw circles
   for the crumbs.

Crumbs	
Ants	

---

4. Each bee gets 1 flower. How many extra flowers are there? [ ]

5. Ring the
   extra flowers.

Flowers	
Bees	

6. Sort the fruit. Record with pictures.
Write how many in each group.

Bananas									
Oranges									

7. Complete the sentences. Ring the word **more** or **fewer**.

There are [ ] **more fewer** bananas than oranges.

There are [ ] **more fewer** oranges than bananas.

8. Sort the vegetables. Record with circles.
Write how many in each group.

Carrots									
Peppers									

9. Complete the sentences. Ring the word **more** or **fewer**.

There are [ ] **more fewer** peppers than carrots.

There are [ ] **more fewer** carrots than peppers.

Organize Categorical Data

Name _____

CA CC Content Standards **1.OA.6, 1.MD.4**
Mathematical Practices **MP.3, MP.6**

I. Look at what Puzzled Penguin wrote.

Am I correct?

Stripes	O	O	O	O	O	O	O	O	O
Spots	O	O	O	O	O				

There are 4 more fish with stripes than with spots.

There are 4 fewer fish with spots than with stripes.

2. Help Puzzled Penguin.

Stripes									
Spots									

There are ☐ more fish with stripes than with spots.

There are ☐ fewer fish with spots than with stripes.

3. Sort the animals. Record with circles.
   Write how many in each group.

Dogs									
Cats									

4. Complete the sentences. Ring the word **more** or **fewer**.

There are [ ] **more fewer** cats than dogs.

There are [ ] **more fewer** dogs than cats.

 PATH to FLUENCY Add.

1. 4
   +3

2. 8
   +1

3. 5
   +5

4. 10
   +0

5. 4
   +6

1. Discuss the data.

2. Write how many in each category.

Eggs Laid This Month

Clucker	◯ ◯ ◯ ◯	_____
Vanilla	◯ ◯ ◯ ◯ ◯ ◯ ◯ ◯ ◯	_____
Daisy	◯ ◯ ◯ ◯ ◯ ◯	_____

Animals in the Pond

Frogs	🐸 🐸 🐸 🐸 🐸 🐸	_____
Fish	🐟 🐟 🐟 🐟 🐟 🐟 🐟	_____
Ducks	🦆 🦆 🦆 🦆	_____

Hot Dogs Sold at the Fair

Eric	🌭 🌭 🌭 🌭 🌭 🌭 🌭 🌭	_____
Miranda	🌭 🌭 🌭 🌭 🌭 🌭 🌭	_____
Adam	🌭 🌭 🌭 🌭 🌭	_____

Watch as each cube is taken from the bag.

3. Draw circles to show how many of each color.

Colors in the Bag									
Red									
Yellow									
Blue									

Use the data to answer the questions.

4. How many red cubes are in the bag? _____

5. How many yellow cubes are in the bag? _____

6. How many blue cubes are in the bag? _____

7. How many more blue cubes are there than red cubes?

_____

8. How many fewer red cubes are there than yellow cubes?

_____

9. There are the most of which color? _____

10. There are the fewest of which color? _____

11. How many cubes are there in all? _____

Data Sets with Three Categories

Name _____

CA CC Content Standards 1.OA.1
Mathematical Practices MP.2, MP.8

VOCABULARY
comparison bars

Solve the story problem.

Use **comparison bars**.

Show your work.

1. Tessa has 15 pens.
   Sam has 9 pens.
   How many more pens
   does Tessa have than Sam?

   ☐
   _____
   label

2. Tessa has 15 pens.
   Sam has 9 pens.
   How many fewer pens
   does Sam have than Tessa?

   ☐
   _____
   label

3. Tessa has 15 pens.
   Sam has 6 fewer pens than Tessa.
   How many pens does Sam have?

   ☐
   _____
   label

4. Sam has 9 pens.
   Tessa has 6 more than Sam.
   How many pens does Tessa have?

   ☐
   _____
   label

Solve the story problem.
Use comparison bars.

Show your work.

---

5. Dan reads 9 books.
Ana reads 11 books.
How many fewer books
does Dan read than Ana?

☐ _____
label

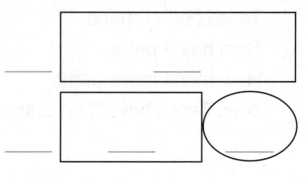

---

6. Luis makes 7 eggs for breakfast.
Emily makes 3 eggs.
How many more eggs
does Luis make than Emily?

☐ _____
label

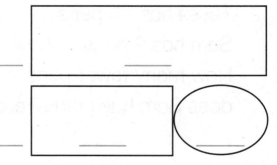

---

7. Noah has 10 more caps than Ben.
Ben has 10 caps.
How many caps does Noah have?

☐ _____
label

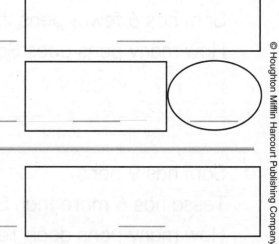

---

8. Jen eats 2 fewer carrots than Scott.
Scott eats 9 carrots.
How many carrots does Jen eat?

☐ _____
label

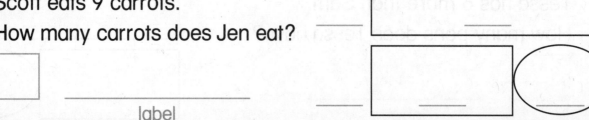

© Houghton Mifflin Harcourt Publishing Company

Name _____

CA CC Content Standards **1.OA.1**
Mathematical Practices **MP.1, MP.4, MP.6**

Solve and discuss.

1. There are 14 tigers and 8 bears. How many more tigers than bears are there?

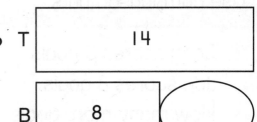

T | 14

B | 8

[ ] _____
       label

$14 = 8 + \boxed{}$

$14 - 8 = \boxed{}$

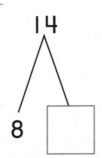

14

8   [ ]

---

2. There are 12 lions. There are 5 fewer camels than lions. How many camels are there?

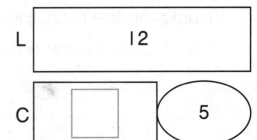

L | 12

C | [ ] | 5

[ ] _____
       label

$5 + \boxed{} = 12$

$12 - 5 = \boxed{}$

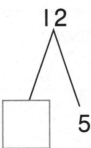

12

[ ]   5

---

3. There are 7 elephants. There are 6 more zebras than elephants. How many zebras are there?

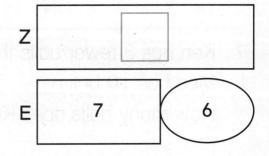

Z | [ ]

E | 7 | 6

[ ] _____
       label

$7 + 6 = \boxed{}$

Solve the story problem.   Show your work.
Use comparison bars.

_____

4. Zach scores 5 goals.
   Jon scores 8 goals.
   How many more goals
   does Jon score than Zach?

   ☐ _____
          label

_____

5. There are 11 cars and 19
   trucks on the road. How many
   fewer cars are there than trucks?

   ☐ _____
          label

_____

6. I see 8 more lilacs than roses.
   I see 9 roses.
   How many lilacs do I see?

   ☐ _____
          label

_____

7. Ken has 3 fewer balls than Meg.
   Meg has 10 balls.
   How many balls does Ken have?

   ☐ _____
          label

Name _____

CA CC Content Standards **1.OA.1, 1.OA.6**
Mathematical Practices **MP.1, MP.4**

Solve the story problem.   Show your work.
Use comparison bars.

1. Cory's cat has 11 kittens.
   Eva's cat has 3 kittens.
   How many fewer kittens does
   Eva's cat have than Cory's?

   ☐ _____
              label

2. There were 3 bicycles here
   yesterday. There are 7 more
   bicycles here today. How many
   bicycles are here today?

   ☐ _____
              label

3. Ms. Perez has 15 horses.
   Mr. Drew has 9 horses.
   How many more horses does
   Ms. Perez have than Mr. Drew?

   ☐ _____
              label

Solve the story problem.
Use comparison bars.

Show your work.

---

4. Jim pops 5 fewer balloons than
Sadie. Jim pops 9 balloons. How
many balloons does Sadie pop?

[ ] _____
       label

---

5. Nick hikes 12 miles in the forest.
Nick hikes 4 more miles than Zia.
How many miles does Zia hike?

[ ] _____
       label

 Subtract.

1.	9	2.	6	3.	8	4.	5	5.	9
	-1		-3		-6		-5		-7

6.	4	7.	10	8.	9	9.	7	10.	6
	-2		-6		-3		-5		-1

11.	8	12.	9	13.	7	14.	10	15.	8
	-7		-4		-7		-5		-1

© Houghton Mifflin Harcourt Publishing Company

Name

CA CC Content Standards **1.OA.1, 1.MD.4**
Mathematical Practices **MP.1, MP.2, MP.4, MP.5**

► Math and the Park

Liam collects data at the park. He wants to
know how many animals can fly and how
many animals cannot fly.

1. Sort the animals.

   Record with circles and 5-groups.

Animals That Can Fly	Animals That Cannot Fly

Use the data to complete.

2. How many animals can fly? _____

3. How many animals cannot fly? _____

4. How many animals does Liam see in all? _____

5. How many more animals can fly than cannot fly?

   _____

Solve.
Show your work.

6. There are 8 swings.
12 children want to swing.
How many children must
wait to swing?

☐ _____

7. 10 bikes are on the rack.
7 children start to ride.
How many bikes do not
have a rider?

☐ _____

1. Sort the bugs. Record with circles.
2. Write how many in each group.

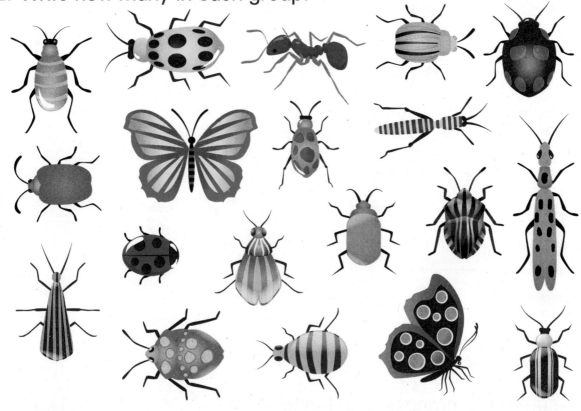

Stripes									
Spots									
Solid									

Use the data. Choose the answer.

3. How many fewer solid color bugs
   are there than bugs with stripes?

   ○ 4   ○ 6   ○ 7

4. How many bugs are there in all?

   ○ 9   ○ 16   ○ 19

5. Sort the fruit. Record with circles.
   Write how many in each group.

Apples								
Bananas								
Oranges								

_____

_____

_____

6. Is the sentence true? Choose Yes or No.

There are more oranges than bananas.　　○ Yes　　○ No
There are more apples than oranges.　　○ Yes　　○ No
There are fewer bananas than apples.　　○ Yes　　○ No

7. How many fewer oranges are there than apples? ☐

8. How many more bananas are there than oranges? ☐

9. How many pieces of fruit are there?

☐ _____
　　　label

Solve the story problem.
Use comparison bars.

10. Rico sees 5 more cats than dogs.
He sees 7 dogs.
How many cats does he see?

☐ _____
label

11. Nori has 15 coins.
Maria has 6 coins.
How many more coins does
Nori have than Maria?

☐ _____
label

Ring the answer. Use comparison bars.

12. Kim picks 13 tulips.
Emily picks 8 tulips.
How many fewer tulips does
Emily pick than Kim?

Emily picks | 5 | fewer tulips than Kim.
            | 8 |
            | 13 |

13. A class is going on a field trip. They collect
data about places to go. Each child votes.
The teacher draws one circle for each vote.

Field Trip Ideas

Park	Zoo	Museum
ooo oo	oooo oooo oo	oo oo

Write two questions about the data.
Answer each question.

Family Letter

Content Overview

Dear Family:

Your child has begun a unit that focuses on measurement and geometry. Children will begin the unit by learning to tell and write time in hours and half-hours on an analog and digital clock.

2:00

hour : minute

Later in the unit, children will work with both 2-dimensional and 3-dimensional shapes.

They will learn to distinguish between defining and non-defining attributes of shapes. For example, rectangles have four sides and four square corners. A square is a special kind of rectangle with all sides the same length. The shapes below are different sizes, colors, and orientations, but they are all rectangles.

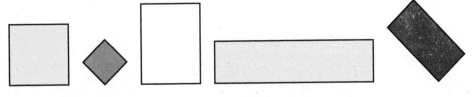

Later in the unit, children will compose shapes to create new shapes.

A cone and a rectangular prism were used to make this new shape.

Children will also learn to partition circles and rectangles into two and four equal shares. They describe the shares using the words *halves*, *fourths*, and *quarters*.

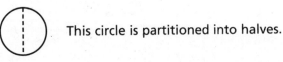

This circle is partitioned into halves.

This circle is partitioned into fourths or quarters.

Children generalize that partitioning a shape into more equal shares creates smaller shares: one fourth of the circle above is smaller than one half of the circle.

Another concept in this unit is length measurement. Children order three objects by length.

These objects are in order from longest to shortest.

They also use same-size length units such as paper clips to measure the length of an object.

This ribbon is 4 paper clips long.

You can help your child practice these new skills at home. If you have any questions, please contact me.

Sincerely,
Your child's teacher

CA CC

Unit 7 addresses the following standards from the *Common Core State Standards for Mathematics with California Additions*: **1.OA.6, 1.MD.1, 1.MD.2, 1.MD.3, 1.G.1, 1.G.2, 1.G.3** and all Mathematical Practices.

Estimada familia:

Su niño ha comenzado una unidad sobre medidas y geometría. Comenzará esta unidad aprendiendo a leer y escribir la hora en punto y la media hora en un reloj analógico y en uno digital.

2:00

hora : minuto

Después, trabajará con figuras bidimensionales y tridimensionales.

Aprenderá a distinguir entre atributos que definen a una figura y los que no la definen. Por ejemplo, los rectángulos tienen cuatro lados y cuatro esquinas. Un cuadrado es un tipo especial de rectángulo que tiene lados de igual longitud. Las figuras de abajo tienen diferente tamaño, color y orientación, pero todas son rectángulos.

Más adelante en la unidad, los niños acomodarán figuras de diferentes maneras para formar nuevas figuras.

 Para formar esta nueva figura se usaron un cono y un prisma rectangular.

También aprenderán a dividir círculos y rectángulos en dos y cuatro partes iguales. Describirán esas partes usando *mitades* y *cuartos*.

 Este círculo está dividido en mitades.

 Este círculo está dividido en cuartos.

Deducirán que si dividen un figura en más partes iguales, obtendrán partes más pequeñas: un cuarto del círculo es más pequeño que una mitad.

Un vistazo general al contenido

Otro concepto que se enseña en esta unidad es la medición de longitudes. Los niños ordenan tres objetos según su longitud.

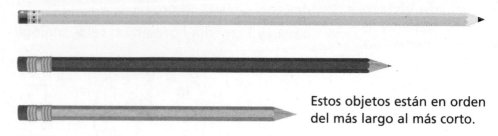

Estos objetos están en orden del más largo al más corto.

También usan unidades de la misma longitud, tales como clips, para medir la longitud de un objeto.

Esta cinta mide 4 clips de longitud.

Usted puede ayudar a su niño a practicar estas nuevas destrezas en casa. Si tiene alguna pregunta, comuníquese conmigo.

Atentamente,
El maestro de su niño

CA CC

En la Unidad 7 se aplican los siguientes estándares auxiliares, contenidos en los *Estándares estatales comunes de matemáticas con adiciones para California*: **1.0A.6, 1.MD.1, 1.MD.2, 1.MD.3, 1.G.1, 1.G.2, 1.G.3** y todos los de prácticas matemáticas.

Student Clock (with hands) **201**

Tell and Write Time in Hours

Class Activity

VOCABULARY
clock

Read the **clock**.

Write the time on the digital clock.

1.

2:00

hour : minute

2.

:

hour : minute

3.

:

4.

:

5.

:

6.

:

7.

:

8.

:

9.

:

10.

:

VOCABULARY
hour hand

Draw the **hour hand** on the clock
to show the time.

11. 4:00

12. 10:00

13. 5:00

14. 8:00

15. Look at the hour hand Puzzled Penguin drew.

3:00

Am I correct?

16. Help Puzzled Penguin.

3:00

Tell and Write Time in Hours

Class Activity

CA CC Content Standards **1.MD.3**
Mathematical Practices **MP.4, MP.7, MP.8**

Clocks for "Our Busy Day" Book

Read the clock.

Write the time on the digital clock.

1.

:

hour : minute

2.

:

hour : minute

3.

:

4.

:

Draw the hour hand on the clock
to show the time.

5.

6:00

6.

9:00

7.

8:00

8.

7:00

9.

4:00

10.

3:00

Fill in the numbers on the clock.

Choose an hour time.

Draw the hands to show the time. Write the time.

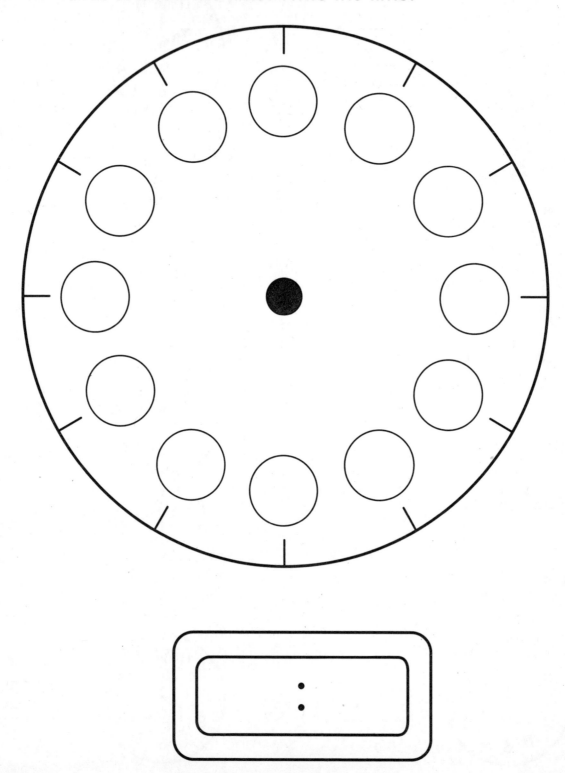

CA CC Content Standards **1.MD.3**
Mathematical Practices **MP.3, MP.6, MP.7**

Name _____

Read the clock.

Write the **half-hour** time on the digital clock.

1.

☐ : ☐
hour : minute

2.

☐ : ☐
hour : minute

3.

☐ : ☐

4.

☐ : ☐

5.

☐ : ☐

6.

☐ : ☐

7.

☐ : ☐

8.

☐ : ☐

9.

☐ : ☐

10.

☐ : ☐

Ring the clock that shows the correct time.
Cross out the clock that shows the wrong time.

11.

7:30

12.

4:30

13.

12:30

14.

9:30

15. Look at the hour hand Puzzled Penguin drew.

1:30

Am I correct?

16. Help Puzzled Penguin.

1:30

Tell and Write Time in Half-Hours

CA CC Content Standards 1.OA.6, 1.MD.3
Mathematical Practices MP.6, MP.7

Name

Show the same half-hour time on both clocks.

1.

2.

3.

4.

5.

6.

7.

8.

9.

Practice Telling and Writing Time **211**

Show the same time on both clocks.

Pick hour and half-hour times.

10. 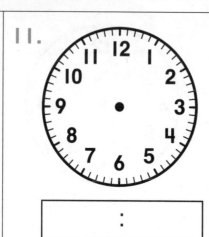 :	11. :	12. 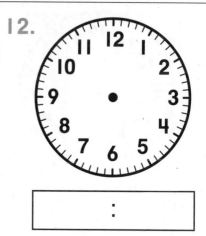 :
13. 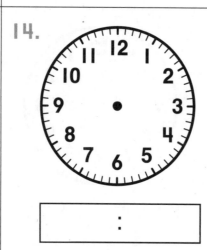 :	14. :	15. 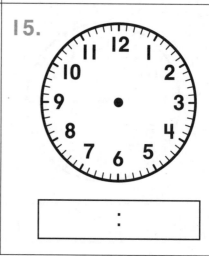 :

○ PATH to FLUENCY **Add.**

1. $7 + 2 = \boxed{}$ 2. $5 + 3 = \boxed{}$ 3. $7 + 1 = \boxed{}$

4. $5 + 5 = \boxed{}$ 5. $8 + 2 = \boxed{}$ 6. $6 + 3 = \boxed{}$

○ PATH to FLUENCY **Find the unknown partner.**

7. $4 + \boxed{} = 8$ 8. $4 + \boxed{} = 10$ 9. $8 + \boxed{} = 9$

Practice Telling and Writing Time

2-Dimensional Shape Set **213**

2-Dimensional Shape Set

2-Dimensional Shape Set **215**

2-Dimensional Shape Set

Name

CA CC Content Standards **1.G.1**
Mathematical Practices **MP.6, MP.7**

I. Which shapes are NOT **rectangles** or **squares**?
Draw an X on each one.

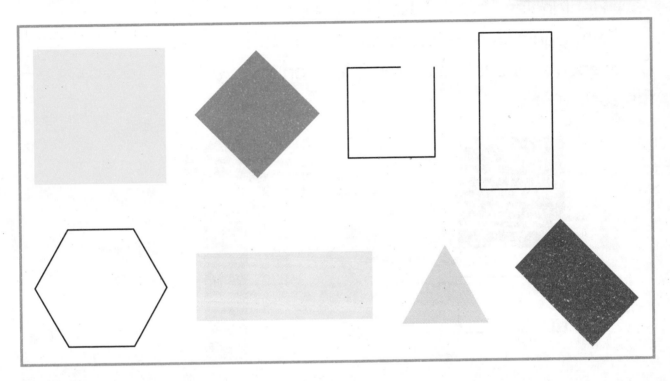

Draw the shape.

2. 4 **sides**,
   4 **square corners**

3. 4 sides the same length,
   4 square corners

4. Sort the shapes into three groups:
   - Squares
   - Rectangles That Are Not Squares
   - Not Squares or Rectangles

Draw each shape in the correct place on the sorting mat.

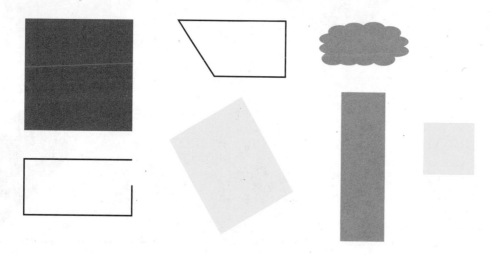

Squares	Rectangles That Are Not Squares	Not Squares or Rectangles

Squares and Other Rectangles

Name

CA CC Content Standards 1.G.1
Mathematical Practices MP.6, MP.7

VOCABULARY
triangles
circles

1. Which shapes are NOT **triangles** or **circles**?
   Draw an X on each one.

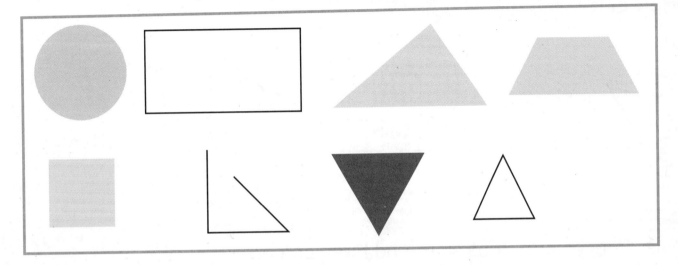

Draw the shape.

2. closed, 3 sides, 3 corners	3. closed, no corners

Name _____

Ring the shapes that follow the sorting rule.
Draw a shape that fits the rule.

4. Shapes that are closed

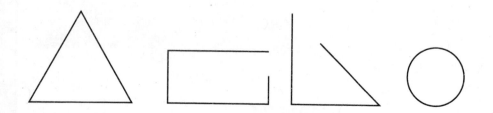

5. Shapes with three sides and three corners

6. Shapes with a square corner

Triangles and Circles

Name _____

CA CC Content Standards **1.OA.6, 1.G.1, 1.G.3**
Mathematical Practices **MP.1, MP.2, MP.4, MP.5, MP.6**

VOCABULARY
halves

Cut out the shapes below.

How many ways can you fold them into **halves**?

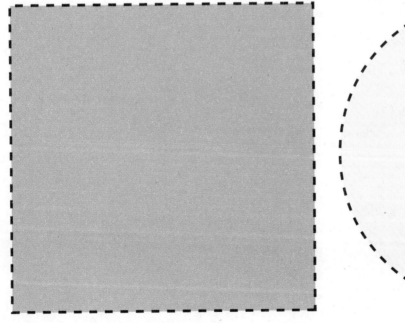

Draw a line to show halves.
Color one **half of** the shape.

1.

2.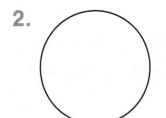

3.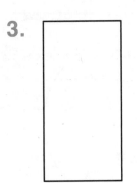

4.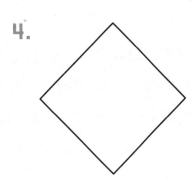

Draw lines to show **fourths**.
Color one **fourth of** the shape.

5.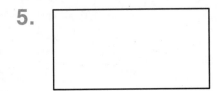

6.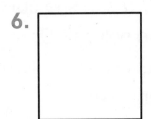

7.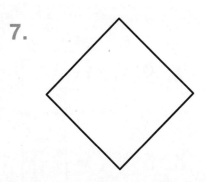

8.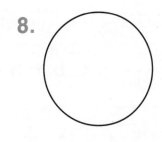

Solve the story problem.

9. Four friends want to share a sandwich. How can they cut the sandwich into four **equal shares**? Draw lines. Color each share a different color.

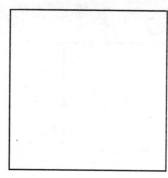

10. The four friends want to share a pie for dessert. How can they cut the pie into four equal shares? Draw lines. Color each share a different color.

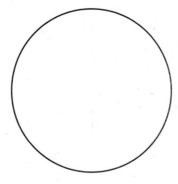

11. One friend only wants one half of her granola bar. How can she cut her granola bar into halves? Draw a line to show two equal shares. Color each share a different color.

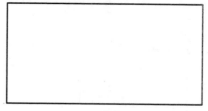

PATH to FLUENCY Subtract.

1. $10 - 3 =$ ☐   2. $8 - 8 =$ ☐   3. $9 - 1 =$ ☐

4. $6 - 5 =$ ☐   5. $7 - 5 =$ ☐   6. $5 - 4 =$ ☐

© Houghton Mifflin Harcourt Publishing Company

Equal Shares

CA CC Content Standards **1.G.1, 1.G.2, 1.G.3**
Mathematical Practices **MP.2, MP.5, MP.6, MP.7, MP.8**

Build and draw the shape.

1. Build a square. Use rectangles.

---

2. Build a rectangle with all sides the same length.
   Use triangles with a square corner.

---

3. Build a rectangle with two short sides and two
   long sides. Use triangles and rectangles.

Use to make the new shape.

4.

7. Use  to make the new shape.

5.

6.

Compose 2-Dimensional Shapes

Name _____

CA CC Content Standards **1.G.1**
Mathematical Practices **MP.6, MP.7**

Shape Names
cone
cube
cylinder
rectangular prism
sphere

Draw a line to match like shapes.
Write the name of the shape.

1.   ○   _____

2.   _____

3.    _____

4. 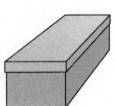   _____

5.   A to Z   _____

Name _____

VOCABULARY
rectangular prisms
cubes

6. Which shapes are NOT **rectangular prisms**?
   Draw an X on each one.

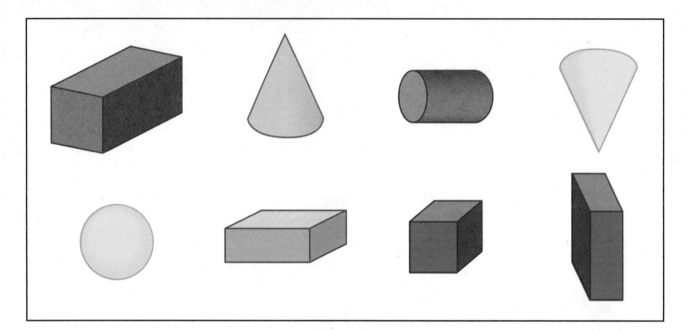

7. Ring the shapes that are **cubes**.

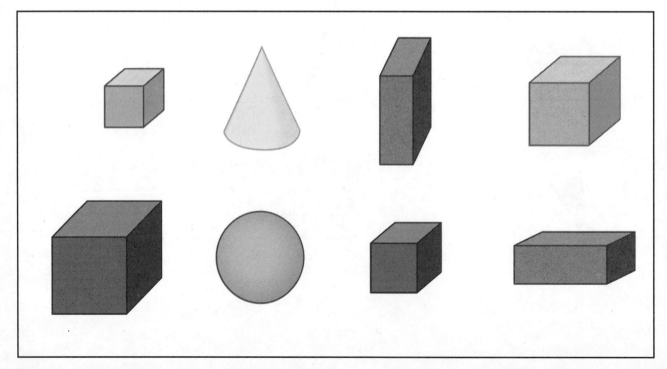

3-Dimensional Shapes

7-11

Class Activity

Name

CA CC Content Standards **1.G.1, 1.G.2**
Mathematical Practices **MP.6**

Ring the shapes used to make the new shape.

1.

2.

3.

4.

5.

Compose 3-Dimensional Shapes **231**

Ring the shape used to make the larger shape.

6.

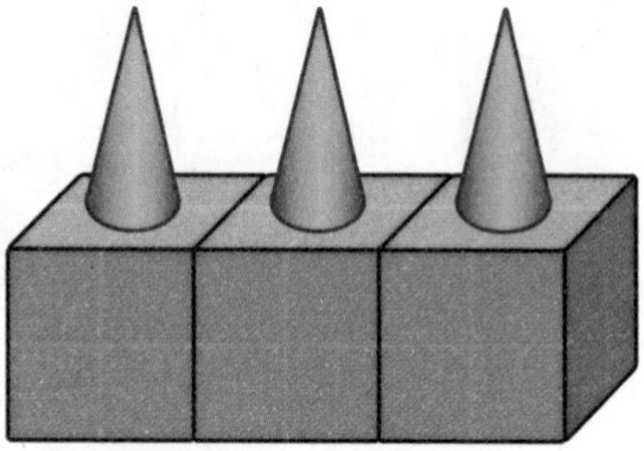

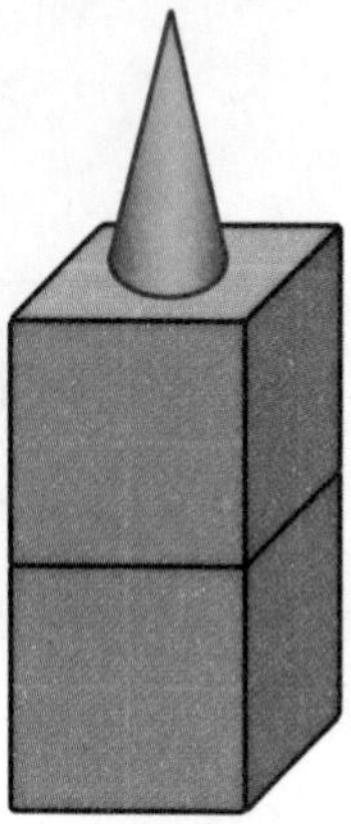

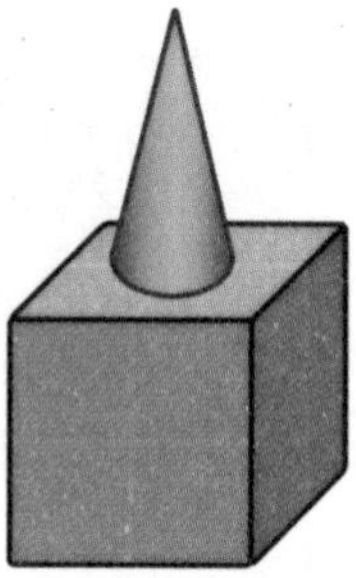

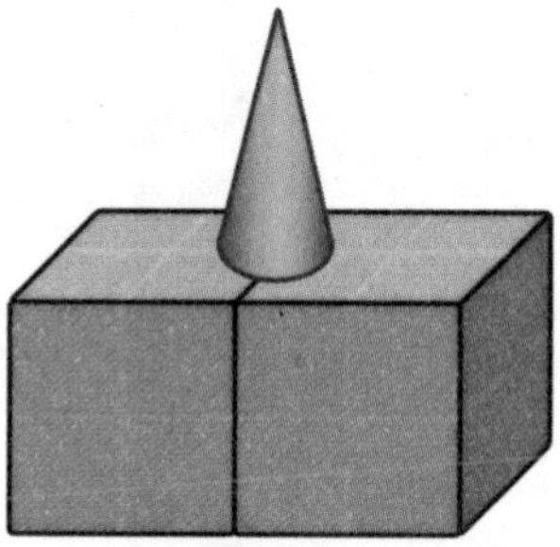

7.

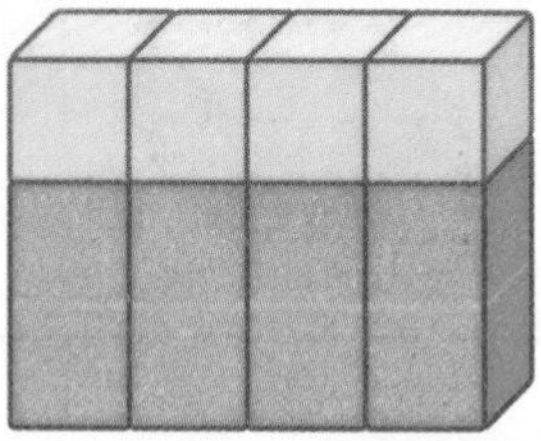

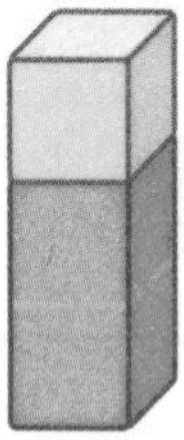

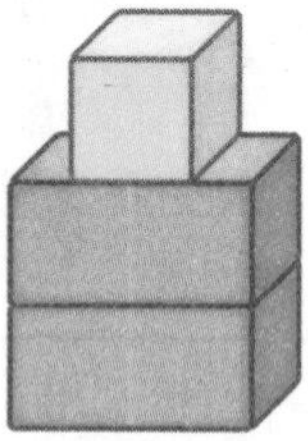

8.

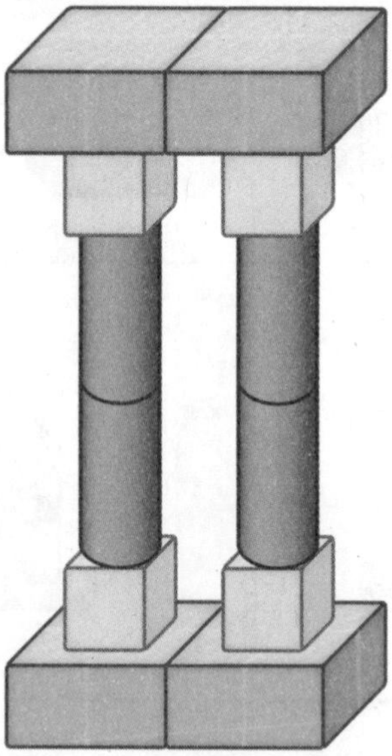

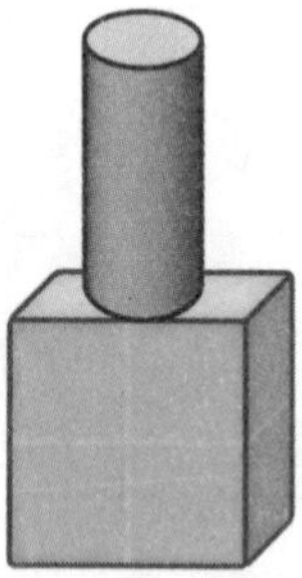

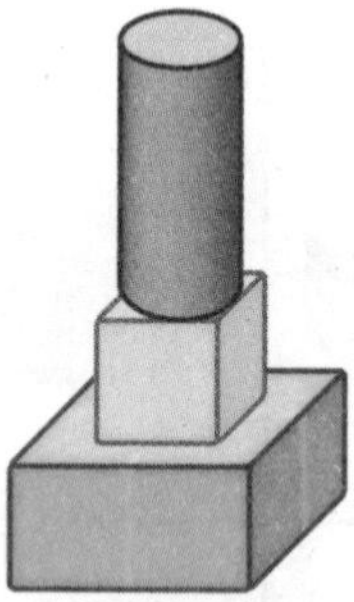

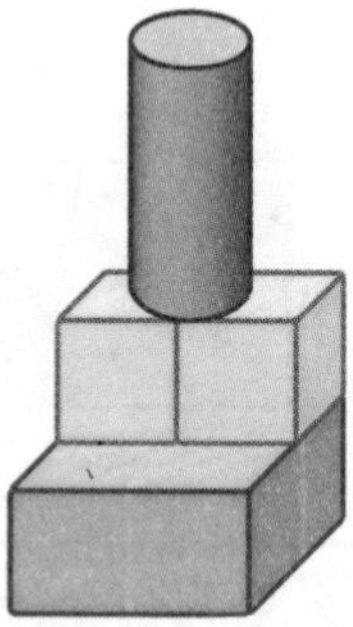

9.

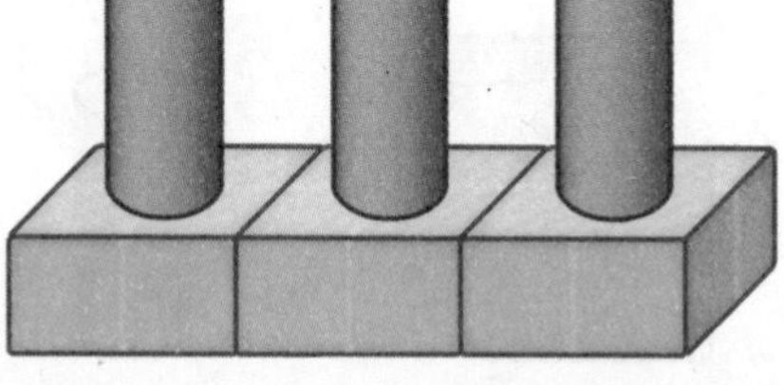

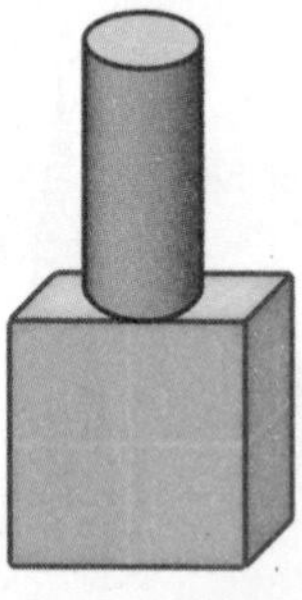

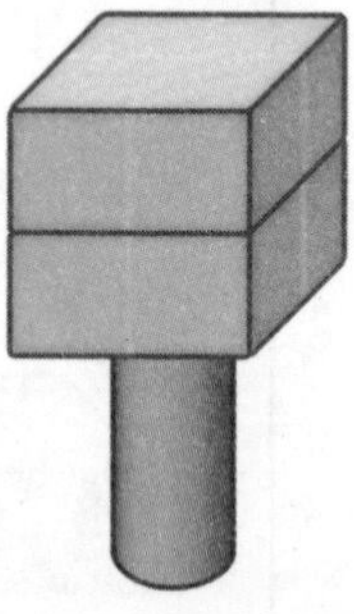

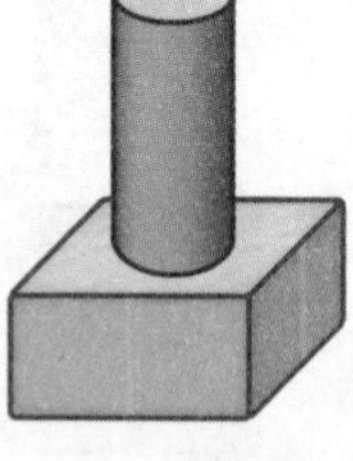

Compose 3-Dimensional Shapes

Name

CA CC Content Standards **1.MD.1**
Mathematical Practices **MP.6**

Write 1, 2, 3 to order from shortest to longest.

1.

☐

☐

☐

2.

☐

☐

☐

Draw three different lines.
Write 1, 2, 3 to order from longest to shortest.

3.

4.

Order by Length

Name _____

CA CC Content Standards **1.OA.6, 1.MD.2**
Mathematical Practices **MP.5**

Measure in paper clips.

1. Red ribbon   How long? ☐ paper clips

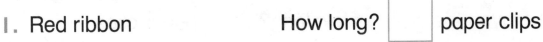

2. Blue ribbon   How long? ☐ paper clips

3. Green pencil   How long? ☐ paper clips

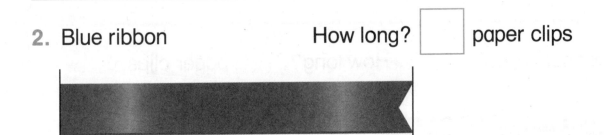

4. Purple pencil   How long? ☐ paper clips

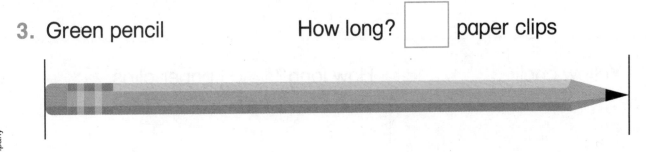

Measure in paper clips.

5. Orange crayon   How long? ☐ paper clips

6. Brown paintbrush   How long? ☐ paper clips

7. Yellow chalk   How long? ☐ paper clips

PATH to FLUENCY Add.

1.	2.	3.	4.	5.
7	2	4	1	0
+3	+6	+5	+7	+9

Name _____

CA CC Content Standards **1.MD.1, 1.MD.2, 1.G.3**
Mathematical Practices **MP.1, MP.2, MP.4, MP.5, MP.6**

► Math and a Picnic

Jay and his family are going on a picnic.
Draw lines to show equal shares.

1. Jay wants to share his burger
   with his mom. How can he cut
   his burger into two equal shares?

2. Jay and his three sisters want
   to share a pan of corn bread.
   How can he cut the bread into
   four equal shares?

3. Jay's mom and his three
   sisters want to share a block of
   cheese. How can they cut the
   block of cheese into four
   equal shares?

There will be lots of food at the picnic.
Measure the food in small paper clips.

4. Orange slice

How long? ☐ paper clips

5. Celery

How long? ☐ paper clips

6. Cracker

How long? ☐ paper clips

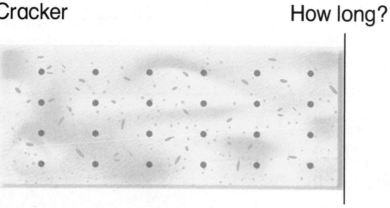

7. Order the picnic food from longest
to shortest. Write the names.

Focus on Mathematical Practices

Name _____

Read the clock.

Write the time on the digital clock.

1.

┌─────────┐
│   :   │
└─────────┘

2.

┌─────────┐
│   :   │
└─────────┘

Draw the hands to show the time.

3. 8:30

4. 3:00

5. Which shapes are NOT triangles?

Draw an X on each one.

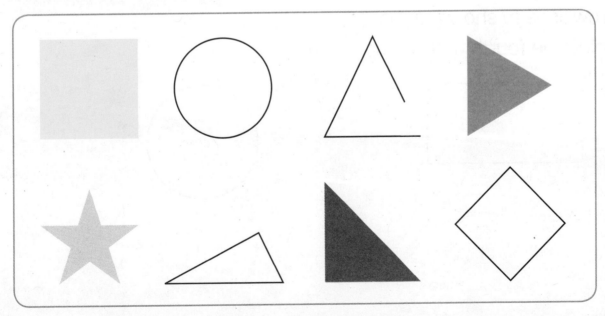

6. Is the shape a square? Choose Yes or No.

○ Yes   ○ No

○ Yes   ○ No

Draw a line to show halves.
Color one half of the shape.

7.
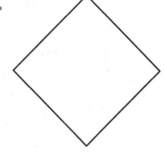

8.
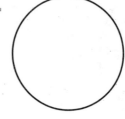

Draw lines to show fourths.
Color one fourth of the shape.

9.
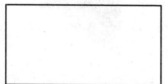

10.
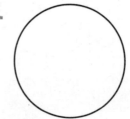

Dear Family:

Your child will be using special drawings of 10-sticks and circles to add greater numbers. The sticks show the number of tens, and the circles show the number of ones. When a new group of ten is made, a ring is drawn around it.

There are several ways for children to show the new group of ten when they add 2-digit numbers.

- Children can do the addition with a single total. The 1 for the new ten can be written either below the tens column or above it. Writing it below makes addition easier because the 1 new ten is added after children have added the two numbers that are already there. Also, children can see the 16 they made from 7 and 9 because the 1 and 6 are closer together than they were when the new ten was written above.

$$\begin{array}{r} 27 \\ + 49 \\ \hline 76 \end{array}$$ new ten below

$$\begin{array}{r} 27 \\ + 49 \\ \hline 76 \end{array}$$ new ten above

- Children can make separate totals for tens and ones. Many first-graders prefer to work from left to right because that is how they read. They add the tens (20 + 40 = 60) and then the ones (7 + 9 = 16). The last step is to add the two totals together (60 + 16 = 76).

$$\begin{array}{r} 27 \\ + 49 \\ \hline 60 \\ 16 \\ \hline 76 \end{array}$$ left to right

$$\begin{array}{r} 27 \\ + 49 \\ \hline 16 \\ 60 \\ \hline 76 \end{array}$$ right to left

You may notice your child using one of these methods as he or she completes homework.

Sincerely,
Your child's teacher

CA CC

Unit 8 addresses the following standards from the *Common Core State Standards for Mathematics with California Additions*: **1.OA.6, 1.NBT.4** and all Mathematical Practices.

© Houghton Mifflin Harcourt Publishing Company

Carta a la familia

Un vistazo general al contenido

Estimada familia:

Su niño usará dibujos especiales de palitos de decenas y círculos para sumar números más grandes. Los palitos muestran el número de decenas y los círculos muestran el número de unidades. Cuando se forma un nuevo grupo de diez, se encierra.

|| ○○○○○ ○○   → ||⌐○○○○○ ○○⌐
|||| ○○○○○ ○○○○ |||| ○○○○○ ○○○○

Hay varias maneras en las que los niños pueden mostrar el nuevo grupo de diez al sumar números de 2 dígitos.

- Pueden hacer la suma con un total único. El 1 que indica la nueva decena se puede escribir abajo o arriba de la columna de las decenas. Escribirlo abajo hace que la suma sea más fácil porque la nueva decena se suma después de sumar los dos números que ya estaban allí. Además, los niños pueden ver el 16 que obtuvieron de 7 y 9 porque el 1 y el 6 están más juntos que cuando la nueva decena estaba escrita arriba.

```
   27
 + 49       nueva
 + 1        decena
 ----       abajo
   76
```

```
   1
   27       nueva
 + 49       decena
 ----       arriba
   76
```

- Pueden hacer totales separados para decenas y para unidades. Muchos estudiantes de primer grado prefieren trabajar de izquierda a derecha porque así leen. Suman las decenas (20 + 40 = 60) y luego las unidades (7 + 9 = 16). El último paso es sumar ambos totales (60 + 16 = 76).

```
   27
 + 49
 ----
   60
   16
 ----
   76
```
de izquierda a derecha

```
   27
 + 49
 ----
   16
   60
 ----
   76
```
de derecha a izquierda

Es posible que su niño use uno de estos métodos al hacer la tarea.

Atentamente,
El maestro de su niño

CA CC

En la Unidad 8 se aplican los siguientes estándares auxiliares, contenidos en los *Estándares estatales comunes de matemáticas con adiciones para California*: **1.OA.6, 1.NBT.4** y todos los de prácticas matemáticas.

© Houghton Mifflin Harcourt Publishing Company

Name _____

CA CC Content Standards **1.NBT.4**
Mathematical Practices **MP.1, MP.2, MP.8**

Uncle David
28 Apples

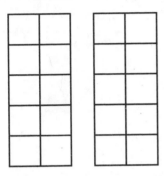

28 apples

16 apples

Put extra apples here.

Aunt Sarah
16 Apples

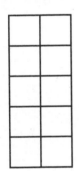

Put extra apples here.

Total Apples

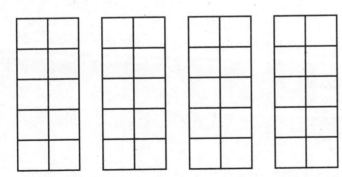

Put extra apples here.

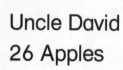

Uncle David
26 Apples

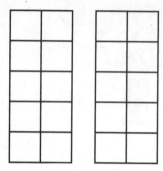

26 apples

20 apples

_____

Put extra apples here.

Aunt Sarah
20 Apples

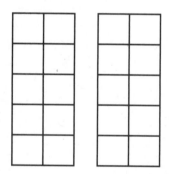

_____

Put extra apples here.

Total Apples

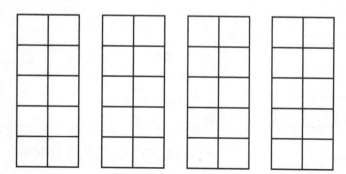

_____

Put extra apples here.

Explore 2-Digit Addition

1. Work in pairs. Each child chooses one apple tree.

2. On your MathBoard or paper, add the apples in the two trees.

3. Check to see if you both got the same answer.

4. Repeat with other trees.

5. Work in pairs. One child chooses one apple tree with a 2-digit number. The other child chooses another tree.

6. On your MathBoard or paper, add the apples in the two trees.

7. Check to see if you both got the same answer.

8. Repeat with other trees.

1. Work in pairs. Each child chooses one peach tree.

2. On your MathBoard or paper, add the peaches in the two trees.

3. Check to see if you both got the same answer.

4. Repeat with other trees.

5. **Discuss** For which problems did you make a new ten?

Add.

6. $\begin{array}{r} 53 \\ + 38 \\ \hline \end{array}$

7. $\begin{array}{r} 16 \\ + 6 \\ \hline \end{array}$

8. $\begin{array}{r} 67 \\ + 15 \\ \hline \end{array}$

9. $\begin{array}{r} 72 \\ + 20 \\ \hline \end{array}$

10. $\begin{array}{r} 56 \\ + 13 \\ \hline \end{array}$

11. $\begin{array}{r} 47 \\ + 30 \\ \hline \end{array}$

12. $\begin{array}{r} 48 \\ + 5 \\ \hline \end{array}$

13. $\begin{array}{r} 82 \\ + 14 \\ \hline \end{array}$

14. $\begin{array}{r} 17 \\ + 2 \\ \hline \end{array}$

Write the vertical form. Then add.

15. $65 + 8$

16. $6 + 73$

17. $56 + 28$

18. $38 + 40$

Discuss Solution Methods

Name

CA CC Content Standards 1.OA.6, 1.NBT.4
Mathematical Practices MP.3, MP.6

Add.

1. 93
    + 6

2. 28
    + 18

3. 66
    + 7

4. 49
    + 30

5. 56
    + 25

6. 15
    + 4

Write the vertical form. Then add.

7. 71 + 19

8. 54 + 20

9. 33 + 29

10. 44 + 4

11. 8 + 74

12. 19 + 67

13. Look at the total Puzzled Penguin wrote.

$$\begin{array}{r} 43 \\ + 39 \\ \hline 712 \end{array}$$

Am I correct?

14. Help Puzzled Penguin.

$$\begin{array}{r} 43 \\ + 39 \\ \hline \end{array}$$

PATH to FLUENCY Add.

1. $5 + 2 = \boxed{}$

2. $7 + 1 = \boxed{}$

3. $3 + 2 = \boxed{}$

4. $\boxed{} = 8 + 2$

5. $\boxed{} = 3 + 6$

6. $\boxed{} = 4 + 3$

7. $5 + 1 = \boxed{}$

8. $6 + 2 = \boxed{}$

9. $5 + 3 = \boxed{}$

10. $\boxed{} = 7 + 2$

11. $\boxed{} = 4 + 2$

12. $\boxed{} = 2 + 1$

▶ **Math and the Grocery Store**

Use the pictures to solve.

1. How many potatoes are there?

49 potatoes   47 potatoes

 potatoes

2. How many cartons of milk are there?

37 cartons of milk   23 cartons of milk

 cartons of milk

3. 20 cartons of milk spill.
   How many cartons of milk are there now?

 cartons of milk

Use the pictures to solve.

4. How many jars of honey are there?

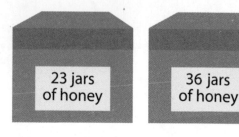

23 jars of honey   36 jars of honey

☐ jars of honey

5. How many jars of jam are there?

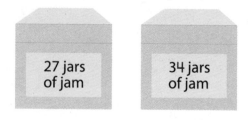

27 jars of jam   34 jars of jam

☐ jars of jam

6. Compare the number of jars of honey to the number of jars of jam. Write the comparison 2 ways.

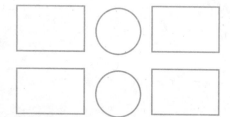

Focus on Mathematical Practices

Solve. Group ones to make tens.

1. Grace has 18 apples.   Jake has 24 apples.

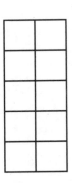 Extra apples   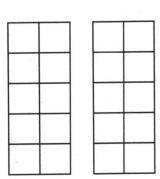 Extra apples

How many apples do they have?

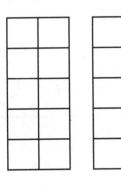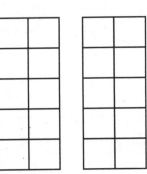   Extra apples

[ ] _____
          label

2. Is the total correct? Choose Yes or No.

$45 + 20 = 47$ ○ Yes   ○ No

$30 + 25 = 55$ ○ Yes   ○ No

$79 + 10 = 89$ ○ Yes   ○ No

$14 + 50 = 74$ ○ Yes   ○ No

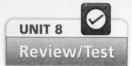
Add.

3.
```
   63
 + 29
```

4.
```
   52
 + 20
```

5.
```
   78
 +  5
```

6.
```
   26
 + 15
```

Write the vertical form. Then add.

7. 28 + 9

8. 45 + 18

9. Choose the totals that equal 55.

   ○ 51 + 4   ○ 46 + 9   ○ 34 + 22   ○ 35 + 20

10. Choose the totals that equal 84.

   ○ 35 + 49   ○ 34 + 44   ○ 42 + 42   ○ 50 + 34

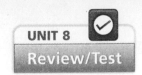
11. How many apples are there?
    Show your work.

54
apples

29
apples

[   ] _____
            label

Choose the correct answer.

12. 57 + 15

   ○ 62

   ○ 68

   ○ 72

   ○ 82

13. 51 + 40

   ○ 55

   ○ 71

   ○ 91

   ○ 95

14. How many peaches are there?
    Show your work.

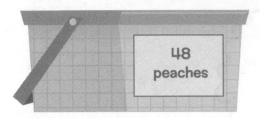

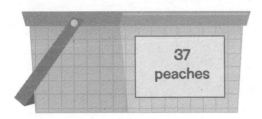

[   ] _____
          label

---

15. Write an addition exercise that you must
    make a new ten to solve. Use two 2-digit
    numbers. Make a Proof Drawing.

Problem Types

	Result Unknown	Change Unknown	Start Unknown
Add To	Six children are playing tag in the yard. Three more children come to play. How many children are playing in the yard now? *Situation and Solution Equation[1]:* $6 + 3 = \square$	Six children are playing tag in the yard. Some more children come to play. Now there are 9 children in the yard. How many children came to play? *Situation Equation:* $6 + \square = 9$ *Solution Equation:* $9 - 6 = \square$	Some children are playing tag in the yard. Three more children come to play. Now there are 9 children in the yard. How many children were in the yard at first? *Situation Equation:* $\square + 3 = 9$ *Solution Equation:* $9 - 3 = \square$
Take From	Jake has 10 trading cards. He gives 3 to his brother. How many trading cards does he have left? *Situation and Solution Equation:* $10 - 3 = \square$	Jake has 10 trading cards. He gives some to his brother. Now Jake has 7 trading cards left. How many cards does he give to his brother? *Situation Equation:* $10 - \square = 7$ *Solution Equation:* $10 - 7 = \square$	Jake has some trading cards. He gives 3 to his brother. Now Jake has 7 trading cards left. How many cards does he start with? *Situation Equation:* $\square - 3 = 7$ *Solution Equation:* $7 + 3 = \square$

[1]A situation equation represents the structure (action) in the problem situation. A solution equation shows the operation used to find the answer.

Problem Types (continued)

	Total Unknown	Addend Unknown	Both Addends Unknown
Put Together/ Take Apart	There are 9 red roses and 4 yellow roses in a vase. How many roses are in the vase? *Math Drawing*[2]:  *Situation and Solution Equation:* $9 + 4 = \square$	Thirteen roses are in the vase. 9 are red and the rest are yellow. How many roses are yellow? *Math Drawing:* 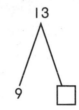 *Situation Equation:* $13 = 9 + \square$ *Solution Equation:* $13 - 9 = \square$	Ana has 13 roses. How many can she put in her red vase and how many in her blue vase? *Math Drawing:* 13 *Situation Equation:* $13 = \square + \square$

[2]These math drawings are called Math Mountains in Grades 1–3 and break-apart drawings in Grades 4 and 5.

	Difference Unknown	Bigger Unknown	Smaller Unknown
Compare[3]	Aki has 8 apples. Sofia has 14 apples. How many **more** apples does **Sofia** have than Aki? Aki has 8 apples. Sofia has 14 apples. How many **fewer** apples does **Aki** have than Sofia? *Math Drawing:* S [14] A [8] (?) *Situation Equation:* $8 + \square = 14$ *Solution Equation:* $14 - 8 = \square$	**Leading Language** Aki has 8 apples. **Sofia** has **6 more** apples than Aki. How many apples does Sofia have? **Misleading Language** Aki has 8 apples. **Aki** has **6 fewer** apples than Sofia. How many apples does Sofia have? *Math Drawing:* S [?] A [8] (6) *Situation and Solution Equation:* $8 + 6 = \square$	**Leading Language** Sofia has 14 apples. **Aki** has **6 fewer** apples than Sofia. How many apples does Aki have? **Misleading Language** Sofia has 14 apples. **Sofia** has **6 more** apples than Aki. How many apples does Aki have? *Math Drawing:* S [14] A [?] (6) *Situation Equation:* $\square + 6 = 14$ *Solution Equation:* $14 - 6 = \square$

[3]A comparison sentence can always be said in two ways. One way uses *more*, and the other uses *fewer* or *less*. Misleading language suggests the wrong operation. For example, it says *Aki has 6 fewer apples than Sofia*, but you have to add 6 to Aki's 8 apples to get 14 apples.

Glossary

5-group

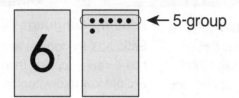

← 5-group

10-group

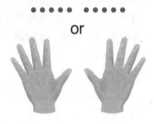

or

10-stick

||| ○○ You can show 32 with three **10-sticks** and two ones.

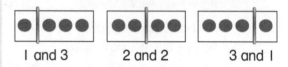

add

3 + 2 = 5

●●● ●●

addend

5 + 4 = 9   5 + 4 + 8 = 17
↑ ↑   ↑ ↑ ↑
addends   addends
(partners)

addition story problem

There are 5 ducks.

Then 3 more come.

How many ducks are there now?

break-apart

You can **break apart** the number 4.

1 and 3   2 and 2   3 and 1

1 and 3, 2 and 2, and 3 and 1 are **break-aparts** of 4.

circle

circle drawing

clock

analog clock

digital clock

12:30

© Houghton Mifflin Harcourt Publishing Company

S4 Glossary

column

1	11	21	31	41	51	61	71	81	91
2	12	22	32	42	52	62	72	82	92
3	13	23	33	43	53	63	73	83	93
4	14	24	34	44	54	64	74	84	94
5	15	25	35	45	55	65	75	85	95
6	16	26	36	46	56	66	76	86	96
7	17	27	37	47	57	67	77	87	97
8	18	28	38	48	58	68	78	88	98
9	19	29	39	49	59	69	79	89	99
10	20	30	40	50	60	70	80	90	100

compare

You can **compare** numbers.

11 is less than 12.

$11 < 12$

12 is greater than 11.

$12 > 11$

You can **compare** objects by length.

The crayon is shorter than the pencil.

The pencil is longer than the crayon.

comparison bars

Joe has 6 roses. Sasha has 9 roses. How many more roses does Sasha have than Joe?

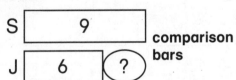

comparison bars

cone

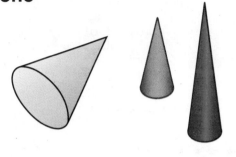

corner

corner

count

count all

$5 + 4 = \boxed{9}$

1 2 3 4 5   6 7 8 9

Glossary (continued)

count on

$$5 + 4 = \boxed{9}$$

$$5 + \boxed{4} = 9$$

$$9 - 5 = \boxed{4}$$

5 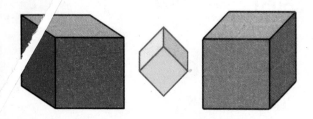 6 7 8 9

Count on from 5 to get the answer.

cube

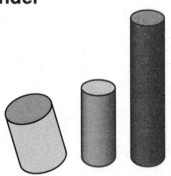

cylinder

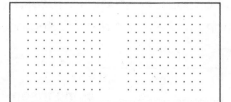

D

data

Colors in the Bag								
Red	○	○	○					
Yellow	○	○	○	○	○	○	○	○
Blue	○	○	○	○	○	○		

The **data** show how many of each color.

decade numbers

10, 20, 30, 40, 50, 60, 70, 80, 90

difference

$$11 - 3 = 8 \qquad \begin{array}{r} 11 \\ -3 \\ \hline 8 \end{array}$$

difference →

digit

15 is a 2-**digit** number.

The 1 in 15 means 1 ten.

The 5 in 15 means 5 ones.

Dot Array

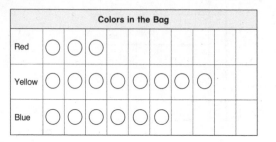

© Houghton Mifflin Harcourt Publishing Company

doubles

4 + 4 = 8

Both partners are the same.
They are **doubles**.

doubles minus 1

7 + 7 = 14, so

7 + 6 = 13, 1 less than 14.

doubles minus 2

7 + 7 = 14, so

7 + 5 = 12, 2 less than 14.

doubles plus 1

6 + 6 = 12, so

6 + 7 = 13, 1 more than 12.

doubles plus 2

6 + 6 = 12, so

6 + 8 = 14, 2 more than 12.

E

edge

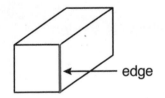
edge

equal shares

2 equal shares   4 equal shares

These show **equal shares.**

equal to (=)

4 + 4 = 8

4 plus 4 is **equal to** 8.

equation

Examples:

4 + 3 = 7   7 = 4 + 3

9 − 5 = 4   4 = 9 − 5

F

face

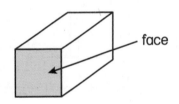
face

fewer

Eggs Laid This Month

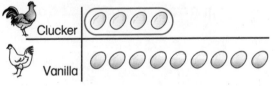

Clucker laid **fewer** eggs than Vanilla.

Glossary (continued)

fewest

Eggs Laid This Month

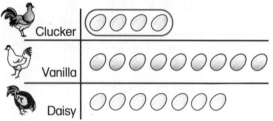

Clucker laid the **fewest** eggs.

fourth of

One **fourth of** the shape is shaded.

fourths

 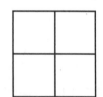

I whole   4 **fourths**, or 4 quarters

G

greater than (>)

34   >   25

34 is greater than 25.

grid

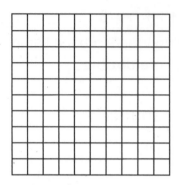

H

half-hour

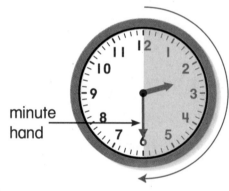

minute
hand

A **half-hour** is 30 minutes.

half of

One **half of** the shape is shaded.

halves

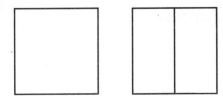

1 whole   2 **halves**

hexagon

hour

hour hand

An **hour** is 60 minutes.

hundred

1	11	21	31	41	51	61	71	81	91
2	12	22	32	42	52	62	72	82	92
3	13	23	33	43	53	63	73	83	93
4	14	24	34	44	54	64	74	84	94
5	15	25	35	45	55	65	75	85	95
6	16	26	36	46	56	66	76	86	96
7	17	27	37	47	57	67	77	87	97
8	18	28	38	48	58	68	78	88	98
9	19	29	39	49	59	69	79	89	99
10	20	30	40	50	60	70	80	90	100

or

||||||||||

K

known partner

$5 + \boxed{} = 7$

5 is the **known partner**.

L

label

We see 9 fish.

5 are big. The others are small.

How many fish are small?

4   _____ fish
label

Glossary (continued)

length

The **length** of this pencil is 6 paper clips.

less than (<)

$$45 \quad < \quad 46$$

45 is less than 46.

longer

The pencil is **longer** than the crayon.

longest

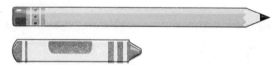

The pencil is **longest**.

M

make a ten

$$8 + 6 = \boxed{}$$

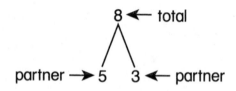

10 + 4 = 14,
so 8 + 6 = 14.

Math Mountain

$$8 \longleftarrow \text{total}$$

partner $\longrightarrow$ 5 $\quad$ 3 $\longleftarrow$ partner

measure

You can use paper clips to **measure** the length of the pencil.

minus (−)

$$8 - 3 = 5 \qquad \begin{array}{r} 8 \\ -3 \\ \hline 5 \end{array}$$

8 **minus** 3 equals 5.

minute

I minute

minute hand

There are 60 **minutes** in an hour.

more

Eggs Laid This Month

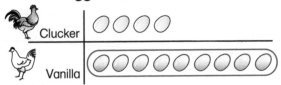

Clucker

Vanilla

Vanilla laid **more** eggs than Clucker.

most

Eggs Laid This Month

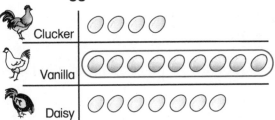

Clucker

Vanilla

Daisy

Vanilla laid the **most** eggs.

N

New Group Above Method

$$\begin{array}{r} {\scriptstyle 1} \\ 56 \\ + \ 28 \\ \hline 84 \end{array}$$ 6 + 8 = 14

The 1 new ten in 14 goes up to the tens place.

New Group Below Method

$$\begin{array}{r} 56 \\ + \ 28 \\ \hline 84 \end{array}$$ 6 + 8 = 14

The 1 new ten in 14 goes below in the tens place.

not equal to (≠)

6 ≠ 8

6 is **not equal to** 8.

number word

12

twelve ← number word

O

ones

ones

56 has 6 **ones**.

order

You can change the **order** of the partners.

7 + 2 = 9

2 + 7 = 9

You can **order** objects by length.

1

2

3

P

partner

5 = 2 + 3

2 and 3 are **partners** of 5.
2 and 3 are 5-**partners**.

partner house

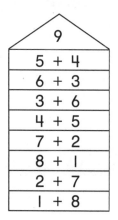

9
5 + 4
6 + 3
3 + 6
4 + 5
7 + 2
8 + 1
2 + 7
1 + 8

partner train

4-train

| 3 + 1 | 2 + 2 | 1 + 3 |

pattern

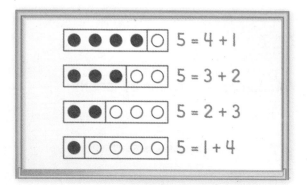

5 = 4 + 1
5 = 3 + 2
5 = 2 + 3
5 = 1 + 4

The partners of a number show a **pattern**.

plus (+)

3 + 2 = 5

$$\begin{array}{r} 3 \\ + 2 \\ \hline 5 \end{array}$$

3 **plus** 2 equals 5.

Proof Drawing

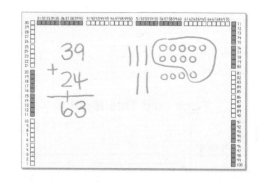

Q

quarter of

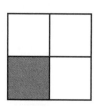

One **quarter of** the shape is shaded.

quarters

1 whole   4 **quarters**, or 4 fourths

© Houghton Mifflin Harcourt Publishing Company

rectangle

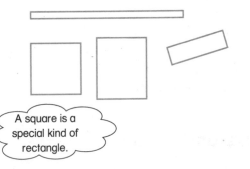

A square is a special kind of rectangle.

rectangular prism

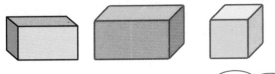

A cube is a special kind of rectangular prism.

row

1	11	21	31	41	51	61	71	81	91
2	12	22	32	42	52	62	72	82	92
3	13	23	33	43	53	63	73	83	93
4	14	24	34	44	54	64	74	84	94
5	15	25	35	45	55	65	75	85	95
6	16	26	36	46	56	66	76	86	96
7	17	27	37	47	57	67	77	87	97
8	18	28	38	48	58	68	78	88	98
9	19	29	39	49	59	69	79	89	99
10	20	30	40	50	60	70	80	90	100

shapes

2-dimensional   3-dimensional

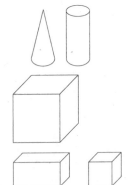

shorter

The crayon is **shorter** than the pencil.

shortest

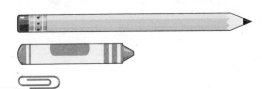

The paper clip is the **shortest**.

Show All Totals Method

$$
\begin{array}{r}
25 \\
+\ 48 \\
\hline
60 \\
13 \\
\hline
73 \\
\end{array}
$$

Glossary (continued)

side

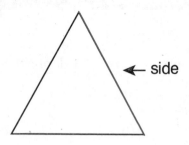

← side

sort

You can **sort** the bugs into groups.

sphere

square

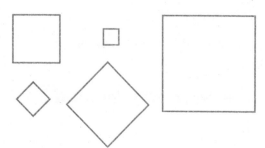

square corner

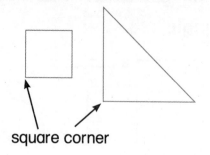

square corner

sticks and circles

1	○
11	| ○
21	|| ○
31	||| ○

subtract

$8 - 3 = 5$

subtraction story problem

8 flies are on a log.
6 are eaten by a frog.
How many flies are left?

switch the partners

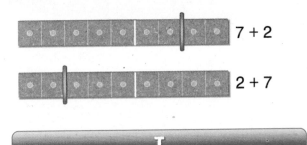

7 + 2

2 + 7

T

teen number

11 12 13 14 15 16 17 18 19

teen numbers

teen total

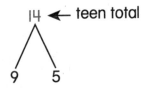

14 ← teen total

9   5

tens

tens

56 has 5 **tens**.

total

4 + 3 = 7

$\begin{array}{r} 4 \\ +3 \\ \hline 7 \end{array}$

total →

trapezoid

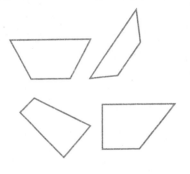

triangle

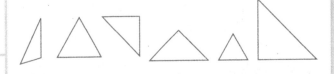

U

unknown partner

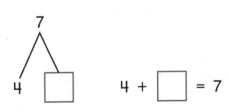

7

4   ☐

4 + ☐ = 7

unknown total

☐

5   3

5 + 3 = ☐

V

vertex

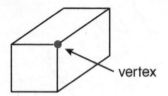

← vertex

vertical form

$$\begin{array}{r} 6 \\ +3 \\ \hline 9 \end{array} \qquad \begin{array}{r} 9 \\ -3 \\ \hline 6 \end{array}$$

Z

zero

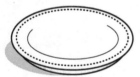

There are **zero** apples on the plate.

California Common Core Standards for Mathematical Content

1.OA Operations and Algebraic Thinking

Represent and solve problems involving addition and subtraction.

1.OA.1	Use addition and subtraction within 20 to solve word problems involving situations of adding to, taking from, putting together, taking apart, and comparing, with unknowns in all positions, e.g., by using objects, drawings, and equations with a symbol for the unknown number to represent the problem.	Unit 1 Lessons 2, 3, 4, 5, 6, 7, 8; Unit 2 Lessons 1, 2, 3, 4, 10, 11, 12, 13, 14, 15, 16; Unit 3 Lessons 2, 4, 5, 6, 7, 8, 9, 10, 11, 12; Unit 4 Lesson 5; Unit 5 Lessons 1, 2, 3, 4, 5, 11; Unit 6 Lessons 1, 2, 3, 4, 5, 6, 7, 8, 9
1.OA.2	Solve word problems that call for addition of three whole numbers whose sum is less than or equal to 20, e.g., by using objects, drawings, and equations with a symbol for the unknown number to represent the problem.	Unit 5 Lessons 6, 11; Unit 6 Lessons 1, 4, 5, 9

Understand and apply properties of operations and the relationship between addition and subtraction.

1.OA.3	Apply properties of operations as strategies to add and subtract.	Unit 1 Lessons 3, 4, 5, 6, 7, 8, 9; Unit 2 Lesson 7; Unit 4 Lesson 5; Unit 5 Lesson 6
1.OA.4	Understand subtraction as an unknown-addend problem.	Unit 3 Lessons 6, 7, 8, 9, 10, 12; Unit 5 Lessons 1, 2, 5

Add and subtract within 20.

1.OA.5	Relate counting to addition and subtraction (e.g., by counting on 2 to add 2).	Unit 1 Lessons 1, 2, 3, 4, 5, 6, 7, 8, 9; Unit 2 Lessons 5, 6, 7, 8, 9; Unit 3 Lessons 1, 3, 4, 6, 7, 11; Unit 4 Lessons 1, 4, 5, 7, 15, 16; Unit 5 Lessons 1, 2, 4 **Quick Practices:** Five Crows in a Row; Giant Number Cards

1.OA.6	Add and subtract within 20, demonstrating fluency for addition and subtraction within 10. Use strategies such as counting on; making ten (e.g., $8 + 6 = 8 + 2 + 4 = 10 + 4 = 14$); decomposing a number leading to a ten (e.g., $13 - 4 = 13 - 3 - 1 = 10 - 1 = 9$); using the relationship between addition and subtraction (e.g., knowing that $8 + 4 = 12$, one knows $12 - 8 = 4$); and creating equivalent but easier or known sums (e.g., adding $6 + 7$ by creating the known equivalent $6 + 6 + 1 = 12 + 1 = 13$).	Unit 1 Lessons 3, 4, 5, 6, 7, 8, 9; Unit 2 Lessons 1, 2, 3, 5, 6, 7, 8, 9, 10, 11, 12, 14, 15, 16; Unit 3 Lessons 1, 3, 4, 5, 6, 7, 10, 11, 12; Unit 4 Lessons 4, 5, 6, 10, 11, 15; Unit 5 Lessons 1, 2, 3, 4, 5, 10, 11; Unit 6 Lessons 3, 8; Unit 7 Lessons 5, 8, 13; Unit 8 Lesson 5 **Daily Routines:** Number Partners; Partner Houses; Mountains and Equations; Add and Subtract Within 10; Add and Subtract Teen Numbers **Quick Practices:** Doubles to 10; Partners of 10; After or the Same? (+1 or +0); Add and Subtract 0; Count on from the Greater Number; After or Before? (+1 or −1); Before or the Same? (−1 or −0); Count On to Find the Unknown Partner; Count On to Subtract; Add Within 10; Unknown Partners Within 10; Double the Bubbles; Partner Pairs

Work with addition and subtraction equations.

1.OA.7	Understand the meaning of the equal sign, and determine if equations involving addition and subtraction are true or false.	Unit 2 Lessons 1, 2, 3, 4, 11, 12, 13, 16; Unit 3 Lesson 12
1.OA.8	Determine the unknown whole number in an addition or subtraction equation relating three whole numbers.	Unit 1 Lessons 3, 4, 5, 6, 7, 8; Unit 2 Lessons 5, 6, 7, 8, 9, 10, 12, 13, 16; Unit 3 Lessons 3, 4, 6, 7, 9, 11, 12; Unit 4 Lessons 4, 5, 10, 11; Unit 5 Lessons 1, 2, 3, 4, 5

1.NBT Number and Operations in Base Ten

Extend the counting sequence.

1.NBT.1	Count to 120, starting at any number less than 120. In this range, read and write numerals and represent a number of objects with a written numeral.	Unit 4 Lessons 1, 2, 7, 8, 9, 10, 11, 15, 16, 18; Unit 5 Lessons 7, 8, 9 **Daily Routine:** Counting Tens and Ones **Quick Practices:** Count 1–10 on the Number Parade; Number Patterns; Listen for Patterns; Count to 100; One More Tiger, One Less Tiger; Count to 120 Starting at Any Number; Count to 120

Understand place value.

1.NBT.2	Understand that the two digits of a two-digit number represent amounts of tens and ones. Understand the following as special cases:	Unit 4 Lessons 1, 2, 3, 4, 7, 8, 9, 10, 11, 12, 13, 14, 16, 17, 18; Unit 5 Lessons 7, 8, 9 **Daily Routine:** Counting Tens and Ones **Quick Practices:** Show Tens and Ones; Flash Tens and Ones
1.NBT.2a	a. 10 can be thought of as a bundle of ten ones — called a "ten."	Unit 4 Lessons 1, 2, 3, 4, 9, 10, 16, 18 **Daily Routine:** Counting Tens and Ones
1.NBT.2b	b. The numbers from 11 to 19 are composed of a ten and one, two, three, four, five, six, seven, eight, or nine ones.	Unit 4 Lessons 2, 3, 4, 5, 8, 10 **Quick Practices:** Number Patterns; Teen Number Flashes; Teen Secret Code Cards
1.NBT.2c	c. The numbers 10, 20, 30, 40, 50, 60, 70, 80, 90 refer to one, two, three, four, five, six, seven, eight, or nine tens (and 0 ones).	Unit 4 Lessons 1, 7, 8, 9, 13, 14, 18; Unit 5 Lesson 10 **Daily Routine:** Counting Tens and Ones **Quick Practices:** Listen for Patterns; Name the Number
1.NBT.3	Compare two two-digit numbers based on meanings of the tens and ones digits, recording the results of comparisons with the symbols >, =, and <.	Unit 4 Lessons 3, 12, 16, 18; Unit 8 Lesson 6 **Daily Routine:** Greater and Less **Quick Practice:** Compare 2-Digit Numbers

Use place value understanding and properties of operations to add and subtract.

1.NBT.4	Add within 100, including adding a two-digit number and a one-digit number, and adding a two-digit number and a multiple of 10, using concrete models or drawings and strategies based on place value, properties of operations, and/or the relationship between addition and subtraction; relate the strategy to a written method and explain the reasoning used. Understand that in adding two-digit numbers, one adds tens and tens, ones and ones; and sometimes it is necessary to compose a ten.	Unit 4 Lessons 9, 10, 11, 13, 14, 15, 16, 17, 18; Unit 5 Lessons 9, 10, 11; Unit 8 Lessons 1, 2, 3, 4, 5, 6 **Daily Routine:** Counting Tens and Ones **Quick Practices:** The Beetle Rhyme; Partner Pairs
1.NBT.5	Given a two-digit number, mentally find 10 more or 10 less than the number, without having to count; explain the reasoning used.	Unit 4 Lesson 1; Unit 5 Lessons 8, 9 **Quick Practices:** The Lion's Den; The Beetle Rhyme
1.NBT.6	Subtract multiples of 10 in the range 10–90 from multiples of 10 in the range 10–90 (positive or zero differences), using concrete models or drawings and strategies based on place value, properties of operations, and/or the relationship between addition and subtraction; relate the strategy to a written method and explain the reasoning used.	Unit 5 Lessons 9, 10, 11; Unit 8 Lesson 6 **Quick Practice:** Subtract Tens

1.MD Measurement and Data

Measure lengths indirectly and by iterating length units.

1.MD.1	Order three objects by length; compare the lengths of two objects indirectly by using a third object.	Unit 7 Lessons 12, 14
1.MD.2	Express the length of an object as a whole number of length units, by laying multiple copies of a shorter object (the length unit) end to end; understand that the length measurement of an object is the number of same-size length units that span it with no gaps or overlaps.	Unit 7 Lessons 13, 14

Tell and write time.

1.MD.3	Tell and write time in hours and half-hours using analog and digital clocks.	Unit 7 Lessons 1, 2, 3, 4, 5, 14 **Daily Routine:** Telling Time **Quick Practice:** Tell Time

Represent and interpret data.

1.MD.4	Organize, represent, and interpret data with up to three categories; ask and answer questions about the total number of data points, how many in each category, and how many more or less are in one category than in another.	Unit 6 Lessons 1, 2, 3, 4, 5, 9

1.G Geometry

Reason with shapes and their attributes.

1.G.1	Distinguish between defining attributes (e.g. triangles are closed and three-sided) versus non-defining attributes (e.g., color, orientation, overall size); build and draw shapes to possess defining attributes.	Unit 7 Lessons 6, 7, 8, 9, 10, 11
1.G.2	Compose two-dimensional shapes (rectangles, squares, trapezoids, triangles, half-circles, and quarter-circles) or three-dimensional shapes (cubes, right rectangular prisms, right circular cones, and right circular cylinders) to create a composite shape, and compose new shapes from the composite shape.	Unit 7 Lessons 9, 10, 11
1.G.3	Partition circles and rectangles into two and four equal shares, describe the shares using the words *halves*, *fourths*, and *quarters*, and use the phrases *half of*, *fourth of*, and *quarter of*. Describe the whole as two of, or four of the shares. Understand for these examples that decomposing into more equal shares creates smaller shares.	Unit 7 Lessons 8, 9, 14

California Common Core Standards for Mathematical Practice

MP.1 Make sense of problems and persevere in solving them.

Mathematically proficient students start by explaining to themselves the meaning of a problem and looking for entry points to its solution. They analyze givens, constraints, relationships, and goals. They make conjectures about the form and meaning of the solution and plan a solution pathway rather than simply jumping into a solution attempt. They consider analogous problems, and try special cases and simpler forms of the original problem in order to gain insight into its solution. They monitor and evaluate their progress and change course if necessary. Older students might, depending on the context of the problem, transform algebraic expressions or change the viewing window on their graphing calculator to get the information they need. Mathematically proficient students can explain correspondences between equations, verbal descriptions, tables, and graphs or draw diagrams of important features and relationships, graph data, and search for regularity or trends. Younger students might rely on using concrete objects or pictures to help conceptualize and solve a problem. Mathematically proficient students check their answers to problems using a different method, and they continually ask themselves, "Does this make sense?" They can understand the approaches of others to solving complex problems and identify correspondences between different approaches.

Unit 1 Lessons 2, 3, 4, 6, 8, 9

Unit 2 Lessons 1, 2, 3, 4, 6, 7, 8, 9, 10, 13, 14, 16

Unit 3 Lessons 1, 2, 3, 4, 6, 7, 8, 9, 10, 11, 12

Unit 4 Lessons 2, 3, 5, 10, 18

Unit 5 Lessons 1, 2, 3, 4, 5, 6, 11

Unit 6 Lessons 1, 2, 4, 6, 7, 8, 9

Unit 7 Lessons 8, 14

Unit 8 Lessons 1, 3, 4, 6

MP.2 Reason abstractly and quantitatively.

Mathematically proficient students make sense of quantities and their relationships in problem situations. They bring two complementary abilities to bear on problems involving quantitative relationships: the ability to *decontextualize*—to abstract a given situation and represent it symbolically and manipulate the representing symbols as if they have a life of their own, without necessarily attending to their referents—and the ability to *contextualize*, to pause as needed during the manipulation process in order to probe into the referents for the symbols involved. Quantitative reasoning entails habits of creating a coherent representation of the problem at hand; considering the units involved; attending to the meaning of quantities, not just how to compute them; and knowing and flexibly using different properties of operations and objects.

Unit 1 Lessons 3, 4, 5, 6, 7, 8, 9

Unit 2 Lessons 1, 2, 3, 4, 6, 10, 11, 12, 13, 15, 16

Unit 3 Lessons 3, 5, 6, 12

Unit 4 Lessons 1, 2, 3, 4, 6, 7, 8, 9, 10, 11, 12, 14, 15, 16, 18

Unit 5 Lessons 1, 2, 3, 4, 5, 9, 10, 11

Unit 6 Lessons 1, 2, 3, 5, 6, 8, 9

Unit 7 Lessons 8, 9, 14

Unit 8 Lessons 1, 2, 3, 4, 5, 6

MP.3 Construct viable arguments and critique the reasoning of others.

Mathematically proficient students understand and use stated assumptions, definitions, and previously established results in constructing arguments. They make conjectures and build a logical progression of statements to explore the truth of their conjectures. They are able to analyze situations by breaking them into cases, and can recognize and use counterexamples. They justify their conclusions, communicate them to others, and respond to the arguments of others. They reason inductively about data, making plausible arguments that take into account the context from which the data arose. Mathematically proficient students are also able to compare the effectiveness of two plausible arguments, distinguish correct logic or reasoning from that which is flawed, and—if there is a flaw in an argument—explain what it is. Elementary students can construct arguments using concrete referents such as objects, drawings, diagrams, and actions. Such arguments can make sense and be correct, even though they are not generalized or made formal until later grades. Later, students learn to determine domains to which an argument applies. Students at all grades can listen or read the arguments of others, decide whether they make sense, and ask useful questions to clarify or improve the arguments.

Unit 1 Lessons 1, 2, 3, 4, 5, 6, 7, 8, 9

Unit 2 Lessons 1, 2, 3, 4, 5, 6, 7, 8, 9, 10, 11, 12, 13, 14, 15, 16

Unit 3 Lessons 1, 2, 3, 4, 5, 6, 7, 8, 9, 10, 11, 12

Unit 4 Lessons 1, 2, 3, 4, 5, 6, 7, 8, 9, 10, 11, 12, 13, 14, 15, 16, 17, 18

Unit 5 Lessons 1, 2, 3, 4, 5, 6, 7, 8, 9, 10, 11

Unit 6 Lessons 1, 2, 3, 4, 5, 6, 7, 8, 9

Unit 7 Lessons 1, 2, 3, 4, 5, 6, 7, 8, 9, 10, 11, 12, 13, 14

Unit 8 Lessons 1, 2, 3, 4, 5, 6

MP.4 Model with mathematics.

Mathematically proficient students can apply the mathematics they know to solve problems arising in everyday life, society, and the workplace. In early grades, this might be as simple as writing an addition equation to describe a situation. In middle grades, a student might apply proportional reasoning to plan a school event or analyze a problem in the community. By high school, a student might use geometry to solve a design problem or use a function to describe how one quantity of interest depends on another. Mathematically proficient students who can apply what they know are comfortable making assumptions and approximations to simplify a complicated situation, realizing that these may need revision later. They are able to identify important quantities in a practical situation and map their relationships using such tools as diagrams, two-way tables, graphs, flowcharts and formulas. They can analyze those relationships mathematically to draw conclusions. They routinely interpret their mathematical results in the context of the situation and reflect on whether the results make sense, possibly improving the model if it has not served its purpose.

Unit 1 Lessons 2, 3, 9

Unit 2 Lessons 1, 2, 10, 13, 16

Unit 3 Lessons 1, 2, 5, 6, 7, 8, 9, 10, 11, 12

Unit 4 Lessons 3, 5, 10, 18

Unit 5 Lessons 1, 2, 3, 4, 6, 11

Unit 6 Lessons 2, 3, 4, 5, 6, 7, 8, 9

Unit 7 Lessons 3, 8, 14

Unit 8 Lessons 1, 2, 3, 6

MP.5 Use appropriate tools strategically.

Mathematically proficient students consider the available tools when solving a mathematical problem. These tools might include pencil and paper, concrete models, a ruler, a protractor, a calculator, a spreadsheet, a computer algebra system, a statistical package, or dynamic geometry software. Proficient students are sufficiently familiar with tools appropriate for their grade or course to make sound decisions about when each of these tools might be helpful, recognizing both the insight to be gained and their limitations. For example, mathematically proficient high school students analyze graphs of functions and solutions generated using a graphing calculator. They detect possible errors by strategically using estimation and other mathematical knowledge. When making mathematical models, they know that technology can enable them to visualize the results of varying assumptions, explore consequences, and compare predictions with data. Mathematically proficient students at various grade levels are able to identify relevant external mathematical resources, such as digital content located on a website, and use them to pose or solve problems. They are able to use technological tools to explore and deepen their understanding of concepts.

Unit 1 Lessons 1, 2, 3, 4, 5, 6, 7, 8, 9

Unit 2 Lessons 5, 6, 8, 16

Unit 3 Lessons 1, 2, 3, 4, 7, 11, 12

Unit 4 Lessons 1, 2, 3, 4, 5, 6, 7, 8, 9, 10, 11, 12, 13, 14, 16, 17, 18

Unit 5 Lessons 1, 2, 6, 7, 8, 9, 10, 11

Unit 6 Lessons 3, 5, 8, 9

Unit 7 Lessons 1, 2, 5, 6, 7, 8, 9, 10, 11, 12, 13, 14

Unit 8 Lessons 2, 3, 6

MP.6 Attend to precision.

Mathematically proficient students try to communicate precisely to others. They try to use clear definitions in discussion with others and in their own reasoning. They state the meaning of the symbols they choose, including using the equal sign consistently and appropriately. They are careful about specifying units of measure, and labeling axes to clarify the correspondence with quantities in a problem. They calculate accurately and efficiently, express numerical answers with a degree of precision appropriate for the problem context. In the elementary grades, students give carefully formulated explanations to each other. By the time they reach high school they have learned to examine claims and make explicit use of definitions.

Unit 1 Lessons 1, 2, 3, 4, 5, 6, 7, 8, 9

Unit 2 Lessons 1, 2, 3, 4, 5, 6, 7, 8, 9, 10, 11, 12, 13, 14, 15, 16

Unit 3 Lessons 1, 2, 3, 4, 5, 6, 7, 8, 9, 10, 11, 12

Unit 4 Lessons 1, 2, 3, 4, 5, 6, 7, 8, 9, 10, 11, 12, 13, 14, 15, 16, 17, 18

Unit 5 Lessons 1, 2, 3, 4, 5, 6, 7, 8, 9, 10, 11

Unit 6 Lessons 1, 2, 3, 4, 5, 6, 7, 8, 9

Unit 7 Lessons 1, 2, 3, 4, 5, 6, 7, 8, 9, 10, 11, 12, 13, 14

Unit 8 Lessons 1, 2, 3, 4, 5, 6

MP.7 Look for and make use of structure.

Mathematically proficient students look closely to discern a pattern or structure. Young students, for example, might notice that three and seven more is the same amount as seven and three more, or they may sort a collection of shapes according to how many sides the shapes have. Later, students will see 7×8 equals the well remembered $7 \times 5 + 7 \times 3$, in preparation for learning about the distributive property. In the expression $x^2 + 9x + 14$, older students can see the 14 as 2×7 and the 9 as $2 + 7$. They recognize the significance of an existing line in a geometric figure and can use the strategy of drawing an auxiliary line for solving problems. They also can step back for an overview and shift perspective. They can see complicated things, such as some algebraic expressions, as single objects or as being composed of several objects. For example, they can see $5 - 3(x - y)^2$ as 5 minus a positive number times a square and use that to realize that its value cannot be more than 5 for any real numbers x and y.

Unit 1 Lessons 1, 2, 3, 4, 5, 6, 7, 8, 9

Unit 2 Lessons 13, 14, 16

Unit 3 Lessons 1, 3, 9, 12

Unit 4 Lessons 1, 2, 3, 5, 6, 7, 8, 9, 10, 13, 17, 18

Unit 5 Lessons 1, 2, 3, 5, 6, 7, 8, 9, 10, 11

Unit 6 Lessons 6, 8, 9

Unit 7 Lessons 1, 2, 3, 4, 5, 6, 7, 9, 10, 11, 14

Unit 8 Lesson 6

MP.8 Look for and express regularity in repeated reasoning.

Mathematically proficient students notice if calculations are repeated, and look both for general methods and for shortcuts. Upper elementary students might notice when dividing 25 by 11 that they are repeating the same calculations over and over again, and conclude they have a repeating decimal. By paying attention to the calculation of slope as they repeatedly check whether points are on the line through (1, 2) with slope 3, middle school students might abstract the equation $(y - 2)/(x - 1) = 3$. Noticing the regularity in the way terms cancel when expanding $(x - 1)(x + 1)$, $(x - 1)(x^2 + x + 1)$, and $(x - 1)(x^3 + x^2 + x + 1)$ might lead them to the general formula for the sum of a geometric series. As they work to solve a problem, mathematically proficient students maintain oversight of the process, while attending to the details. They continually evaluate the reasonableness of their intermediate results.

Unit 1 Lessons 1, 2, 3, 4, 5, 6, 7, 8, 9

Unit 2 Lessons 6, 7, 8, 11, 14, 16

Unit 3 Lessons 8, 9, 12

Unit 4 Lessons 1, 2, 5, 6, 7, 9, 10, 12, 13, 14, 15, 17, 18

Unit 5 Lessons 1, 2, 4, 5, 6, 7, 8, 9, 10, 11

Unit 6 Lessons 1, 6, 7, 9

Unit 7 Lessons 3, 6, 7, 8, 9, 10, 12, 14

Unit 8 Lessons 1, 2, 4, 6

Index

© Houghton Mifflin Harcourt Publishing Company

Counting

count on, 41–42, 43–44, 49–50, 125, 128

Hundred Grid, 163

number words, 115–116

read and write numerals, 25, 115–116, 129–130, 161–162

represent a set with a written numeral, 33–34, 101, 157–158, 177–178

tens and ones, 101, 116, 117, 129–130, 157–158

to 10, 25

Count-On Cards, 45–46, 73–74, 81–82

Cube, 229–230, 231–232

Cylinder, 229–230, 231–232

Data

ask and answer questions, 175, 177–178, 179–180, 184, 191

comparison bars, 185–186, 187–188, 189–190, 192

discuss, 183

interpret, 177–178, 179–180, 181–182, 183–184, 191

mark schemes, 177–178, 191

matching drawings, 179, 192

organize, 175, 177–178, 179–180, 181–182, 183–184, 191

represent, 177–178, 179–180, 181–182, 184, 191

three categories, 178, 183–184

two categories, 175, 177, 179–180, 181–182, 191

Doubles. *See* Addition; Numbers.

Edges, 229–230

Equal shares

fourths, 223–224, 226, 237

halves, 221, 223–224, 226, 237

manipulatives, 221–222

partition into, 223–224

quarters, 223–224, 226, 237

Equations. *See* Algebra.

Family Letter, 1–2, 5–6, 9–12, 31–32, 39–40, 65–66, 99–100, 103–104, 135–136, 159–160, 173–174, 197–200, 243–244

Fluency practice. *See* Addition; Subtraction.

Focus on Mathematical Practices, 25–26, 59–60, 93–94, 129–130, 167–168, 191–192, 237–238, 253–254

G

Geometry. *See also* Equal shares.

attributes
  closed, 219–220
  corners, 217, 219–220, 226
    square corners, 217, 220, 226
  edges, 229–230

© Houghton Mifflin Harcourt Publishing Company

Index (continued)

R

S